Ideal Lambeth

ENTER THE
DREAM-HOUSE

For Geoff –

With my very best wishes,
always –

Happy Christmas 2015!

Tony Hall

(pages 76-81 and 170-173)

BAFTA November 25th 2015

ENTER THE
DREAM-HOUSE

Memories of Cinemas in South London from the Twenties to the Sixties

Edited by Margaret O'Brien and Allen Eyles

Museum of The Moving Image - A Division of The British Film Institute

The British Film Institute exists to encourage the development of film, television and video in the United Kingdom and to promote knowledge, understanding and enjoyment of the culture of the moving image. Its activities include The National Film Archive; The National Film Theatre; The London Film Festival; The Museum of the Moving Image; the production and distribution of film and video; Library and information services; Stills, Posters and Designs; Research; Publishing and Education; and the monthly Sight and Sound magazine.

The Museum of the Moving Image (MOMI) is a division of the British Film Institute.

DIRECTOR: Wilf Stevenson
CONTROLLER BFI SOUTH BANK: Jürgen Berger
CURATOR MOMI: Leslie Hardcastle OBE

DESIGN: A. D. Creative Consultants
        The Royal Victoria Patriotic Building
        Trinity Road London SW18 3SX
        Telephone: 081 870 8743

PRINTED BY: The KPC Group, London and Ashford, Kent

© Copyright Museum of the Moving Image, 1993
ISBN 0-85170-395-X

Museum of the Moving Image
South Bank
Waterloo London SE1 8XT

Overleaf: Opening day at the Astoria Streatham June 1930

ENTER THE DREAM HOUSE

Memories of Cinemas in South London from the Twenties to the Sixties

CONTENTS

We wish to thank the twenty-six participants who made this book possible. Their generosity and enthusiasm made its production a pleasant task.

Thanks also to the following who contributed valuable insights on other areas: Ellen Cobden, Peter Howden, Eric and Ivy Ivens, Bob Morgan, Kenneth Rive and Frances Walker.

For practical help and critical comments along the way, thanks to Marysia Lachowicz, MOMI Education, and to Gill Bailey, Michael Comber, Jim Cook, Eric Crossley, Rhona Hosking, Isa and Roman Lachowicz, Andy Medhurst and Margaret Peach.

Thanks also to the Battersea District Library and Local History Library for their excellent reference facilities and general helpfulness.

The first stage of this project was made possible through research leave granted to Margaret O'Brien by the Research and Information Division of the British Film Institute.

Finally, special thanks to Linda Wood for her meticulous transcriptions of the interview tapes. The final text is enhanced by her knowledge of, and engagement with, the subject.

Illustrations

Special Photography

James Braund took the photographs of Lucy Glide (p14), Leslie Wilkinson (p17), Leslie and Peggy Smith (p20), Bill Halle (p23), Sid Cove (p29), Vi Turner and Fred Creasey (p32), Len England (p36), Clifford Gentle (p42), Leslie Hardcastle (p47), Daisy Moore (p50), Norman Cobden (p54), Mo Heard (p63), Allen Eyles (p67), Moira Mulholland (p74), Tony Sloman (p76), Aine O'Halloran (p82), Albert Critoph (p97), Norman Waring (p107), Joan Howard (p124), Charles Beddow (p129) and Eva O'Rourke (p155).

Tom Stockill took the photographs of Bertha Downes (p26), Denis Norden (p39), Suzanne Waite (p59) and Ellen Bailey (p120).

General Illustrations

We are also most grateful to the following individuals and organisations for the loan or provision of illustrations.

Courtesy of Ellen Bailey: photograph (p122)

Courtesy of Cinema Theatre Association: photograph of Trocadero Elephant and Castle (p168) by the late John Squires

Courtesy of Sid Cove: back cover, and illustration from opening brochure of Gaumont Palace Peckham (p30)

Courtesy of Albert Critoph: photographs on p98 and top right on p101

Copyright © Allen Eyles: photographs of Gaumont Clapham (p54), New Victoria and Victoria Station Cartoon Theatre (both p83), Biograph Victoria (p86), Odeon Chelsea (p137), Odeon Elmers End and Savoy Wandsworth (both p169)

Copyright © David Freeman: photographs of Essoldo Camberwell (p58) and Classic Tooting Bec (p108)

Courtesy of Rhona Hosking: photographs of the Ideal Lambeth (p51 and first title page)

Courtesy of Lambeth Archives: photographs of Golden Domes Streatham (p18) and Pyke's Clifton Hill (p78)

Courtesy of John H. Meredith: photograph of Golden Domes Streatham (p112)

Courtesy of Tony Moss: photographs of Gaumont Palace Peckham (p88 and 89), Canterbury Music Hall (p91) and Quentin Maclean (p102)

Courtesy of Odeon Streatham: photographs on title page, p21 and 37

Courtesy of Positive Pastimes (Patrick Loobey): photograph of Imperial Clapham Junction (p101)

Other illustrations courtesy of BFI Stills, Posters and Designs and the collection of Allen Eyles

Enter the dream-house, brothers and sisters, leaving
Your debts asleep, your history at the door:
This is the home for heroes, and this loving
Darkness a fur you can afford
                    From 'Newsreel' (1938) by C. Day Lewis

This book uses people's memories to recreate going to the pictures and working in cinemas in the period from the Twenties to the Sixties when film, "the great social habit", was the dominant mass medium in Britain.

Some of the recollections go back to the Twenties when cinema took over from the music hall and theatre as the most popular form of entertainment. Most of the memories are of the Thirties and Forties when cinema-going was at its height, reaching a peak of 1,650 million admissions in 1946, when 73% of the population were cinema-goers, nearly half of them going once a week or more. Cinema visits declined in the Fifties but, as the interviews indicate, film-going remained a significant social activity, especially for young people. The average attendance of once every two weeks compares dramatically with the current figure of twice yearly.

Given that film as a major leisure activity and an art form was central to so many people's experiences, it is surprising that the study of cinema audiences has only recently been considered a worthy object of investigation by film theorists and historians. Fortunately there is now an increasing recognition that film can fruitfully be studied and understood in relation to its mass audience.

The twenty-six interviews featured here provide valuable insights for anyone interested in the history of cinema, whether for the purpose of systematic study or for more nostalgic reasons. Collectively they provide a wealth of vivid and fascinating detail, some of it forgotten and undocumented, of the key period of cinema history. We are not claiming that these memories can be totally without distortions, gaps and exaggerations. Recounting memories - that is, the telling of stories about the past from the vantage point of the present - is always to some extent an imaginative reconstruction. But we believe that the memories collected here can and do provide much reliable detail to add to the historical record. However, that is not their only value. These recollections provide more than factual detail. Just as importantly, they convey a sense of the atmosphere, feelings and textures that were particular to the cinema experience in its heyday.

The accounts which follow are more than nostalgic re-creations of past pleasures. Descriptions of everyday life at work or in leisure time are always particularly vivid when recalling childhood and young adulthood. And the memories provide not only a flavour of cinemas and cinema-going but also a sense of the social context, of a society which in this period was undergoing profound social and cultural changes, particularly in the war years.

The people featured in this project, interviewed in 1991 or 1992, comprise a varied group obtained through work and family contacts and an advertisement in the South London Press. They are not, nor are they intended to be, a representative sample of the cinema-going public of the period. For example, of the twenty six, only eleven are women in spite of the fact that women were dominant in the mass cinema audience until the Fifties. Some of the reminiscences come from people who simply enjoyed the cinema without taking it too seriously. Others worked in cinemas simply because it was a job. But, for a significant group interviewed here, the cinema cast a spell leading to careers in the projection box, management, film editing and film journalism.

All the people interviewed are connected to part of South London (Lambeth, Wandsworth, Southwark and adjacent areas) through upbringing and/or work. We have also included the occasional foray into rural, small town or West End cinemas occasioned by life's movements or in pursuit of the art house film. We hope these will provide interesting points of comparison.

South London was chosen for particular reasons, not least because the Museum of the Moving Image, which provided the impetus for this project, is situated there alongside the National Film Theatre on London's South Bank. The area we have covered stretches from the inner city to suburbia and was densely populated with cinemas, many of them the lavish suburban picture palaces of the Thirties which provide a vivid contrast with the converted music halls and fleapits that were also found in the poorer parts of South London.

The memories share common locations and cinemas but also reveal the social contrasts contained within a relatively small area of London. Those who lived in the crowded tenements of the Elephant and Castle inhabited a very different world from those who lived in the new detached houses of Thirties Streatham.

Each person's full interview lasted about one hour and followed a biographical shape. However, we had special areas of interest which we wished to pursue and in the subsequent process of editing the transcripts were "chopped up" under particular headings. This may account for any occasional jumps in the text.

The edited interviews are divided into three main sections: Being There, the medley of experiences which comprised cinema-going; Working There, accounts of work processes and work relationships in cinemas; and Film Talk, memories of and reflections on the world of film, including genres, stars and fandom. The sections are not intended to be hard and fast categories. Each interview developed its own rhythm and style and there is often overflow from one section into another.

Some of the people had something to contribute to two or three areas while others appear only once. Sometimes two or more accounts are printed of the same work procedure such as the handling of change-overs in the projection room or of similar responses to events like air raids. We have included them not only to corroborate the authenticity of the accounts but also because each person recreates and reflects on the past in their own individual way. Where necessary, our questions appear in the text. At other times they have been eliminated to provide a continuous commentary.

Taken all together, we hope that these twenty-six accounts offer a comprehensive and unique recollection of the way it was when "going to the pictures" was a memorable occasion, a taste of luxury and an escape into fantasy.

Note on Pre-Decimal Currency and Film Certificates

There are many references to prices of admission, etc., in pre-decimal days. One present penny is the approximate equivalent of two-and-a-half old pence. Five pence today are the equivalent of the old twelve pence known as a shilling. The old one shilling-and-sixpence is worth seven-and-a-half new pence. A pound is still a pound but it used to be worth twenty shillings or 240 pence. Typical evening admission prices at a leading South London cinema showing new circuit releases in the late Thirties were:

front stalls: sixpence

back stalls: one shilling

back circle: one shilling-and-sixpence

front circle: two shillings

British Board of Film Censors' certificates referred to in the text:

"U" - films passed for universal exhibition,
i.e. no age restriction

"A" - children under sixteen admitted only when
accompanied by an adult (supposed to be a
parent or guardian)

"H" - films with horrific content, restricted to
persons over the age of sixteen (introduced
on 1 January 1937, withdrawn at the end of 1950)

"X" - replaced the "H" certificate from 1 January 1951
and applied more widely to films of adult content, again
restricted to persons over sixteen years of age.

This map shows the relative positions of the South London Cinemas principally recalled in the book's interviews. It does not show the many other cinemas that were not mentioned or only referred to in passing. A few of the South London Cinemas remembered are outside the area shown here

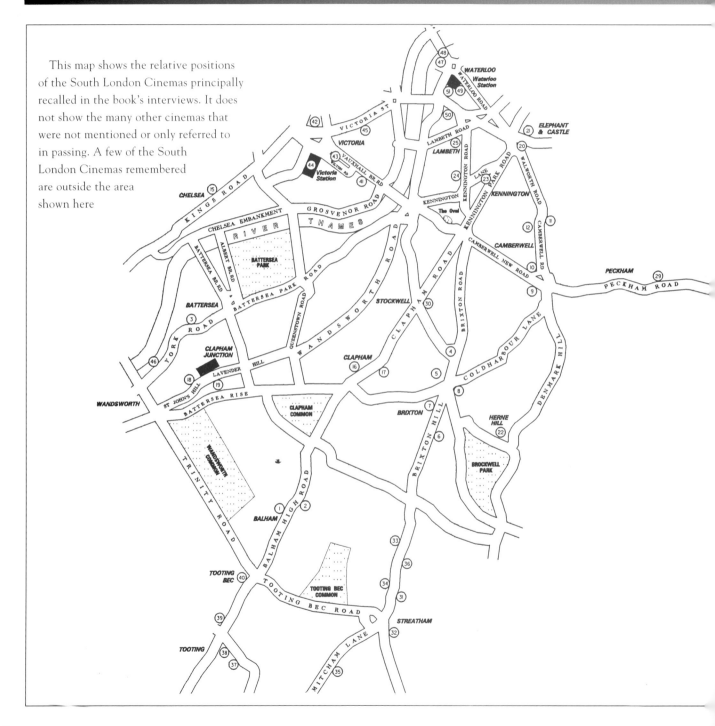

Key to Cinemas

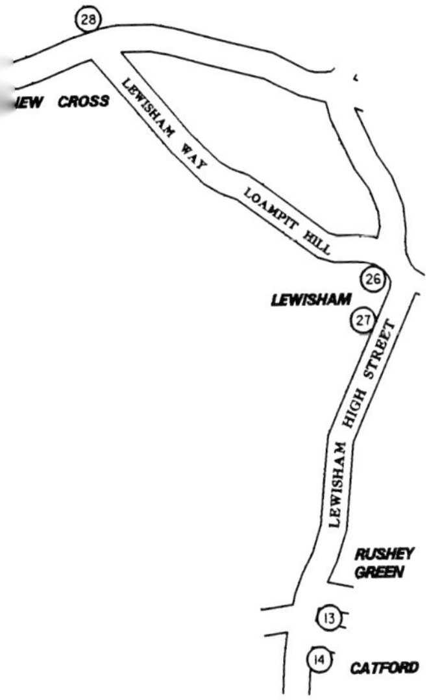

Balham
1. Picture House / Ritz
2. Gaumont

Battersea
3. Super Palace

Brixton
4. Astoria
5. Empress / Granada
6. New Royalty / Clifton
7. Palladium / Regal / ABC
8. Pavilion / Pullman / Classic / Little Bit Ritzy / Ritzy

Camberwell
9. Golden Domes / Essoldo
10. Grand
11. Purple Picture Palace
12. Regal / ABC

Catford
13. Eros and Queens / Gaumont (adjacent)
14. Plaza / ABC / Cannon

Chelsea
15. Gaumont / Odeon

Clapham
16. Majestic / Gaumont
17. Pavilion

Clapham Junction
18. Granada
19. Imperial / Ruby

Elephant & Castle
20. Theatre / ABC / Coronet
21. Trocadero

Herne Hill
22. Grand / Pullman

Kennington
23. Princess
24. Regal / Granada

Lambeth
25. Ideal

Lewisham
26. Gaumont Palace / Gaumont / Odeon
27. Prince of Wales

New Cross
28. Kinema / Gaumont

Peckham
29. Gaumont Palace / Gaumont

Rushey Green - see Catford

Stockwell
30. Ritz / Classic

Streatham
31. Astoria / Odeon
32. Empire
33. Gaumont Palace / Gaumont
34. Golden Domes
35. Mitcham Lane Picture Palace
36. Regal / ABC / Cannon

Tooting
37. Astoria
38. Granada
39. Vogue

Tooting Bec
40. Classic

Victoria
41. Biograph
42. Cameo & Metopole (almost adjacent)
43. New Victoria (Apollo Theatre)
44. Station News Theatre / Cartoon Cinema
45. Strutton Ground Cinema (Army & Navy)

Wandsworth
46. Savoy

Waterloo
47. National Film Theatre (ex Telekinema)
48. National Film Theatre
49. Station News Theatre

Westminster
50. Canterbury
51. Gatti's

Map **11**

Being There

The reminiscences in this section support Roger Manvell's observation in 1944 that "there is more in cinema-going than seeing films. There is going out at night, the sense of relaxation combined with the sense of fun and excitement". The sheer value-for-money, sense of occasion and group feeling that going to the pictures represented in difficult times when there were few alternative leisure activities is evident here.

The interviews reveal many aspects of cinema-going which are far removed from today's experiences. The earlier cinemas were very much social centres performing more functions than the screening of films. Civic openings of these new cinemas were important local events, as were special publicity stunts for new films. The element of live entertainment, for a generation not long removed from the music hall, was much stronger and people recall variety 'turns', organ interludes and community singing. As today, eating was an important part of the viewing experience! Cinema cafes in the large cinemas provided both meals and an ambience that matched the smart and sometimes extravagant style of the auditorium.

Queueing, often recalled in fond terms, features strongly in these reminiscences - not surprisingly since it has been estimated that anyone who went to the cinema twice a week in 1943 might have spent 100 hours queueing to get in. For the young, more unorthodox ways of getting in - "bunking in" through the side exits - were seemingly very frequent. Children would also ask adults to take them into "A" certificate films, with little apparent risk of being pestered.

It is important to remember that new films normally had runs of six days or less, and keen filmgoers had to catch them while they were around, unlike today when hit films run as long as audience demand holds up. Films were not held longer in the past because cinemas cultivated regular weekly visits from their patrons and were not then subdivided to provide several choices of programme. Usually, old films were shown on Sundays, obtained at low rentals, to keep costs down as there was a charity levy on takings and staff had to

be paid higher rates of pay. A standard programme consisted of two features and full supporting programme while Saturday morning pictures for children consisted of a film, serials, shorts and often talent shows and singing.

There were several different types of cinema in the area of South London principally remembered here. New films usually opened in the West End and there were pre-release cinemas at Victoria - the New Victoria and Metropole. The most important local cinemas were the large circuit houses, usually built in the late Twenties or the Thirties and operated by one of the major groups: ABC (Associated British Cinemas), Gaumont, Odeon, or Granada. The American Paramount film company operated three large Astorias at Brixton, Streatham and Old Kent Road in South London until Odeon took them over in the late Thirties, while the Hyams Brothers ran a small circuit of super cinemas including the Elephant and Castle Trocadero and the Metropole Victoria that later became part of the big chains. The Metropole was a pre-release cinema (and later a road-show cinema) while the circuit cinemas further out showed their own circuit's release after presentation in North London. The really big picture palaces usually offered a few live variety acts in the Thirties and had organists to play special interludes.

Other cinemas - usually the older, smaller ones - played reissues and the less desirable new pictures. The Classic Tooting Bec established a strong reputation as part of a chain of enterprising repertory cinemas. Art cinemas were essentially located in the West End, although the National Film Theatre was established on the South Bank at Waterloo. The spread of news theatres was a little wider: they were also to be found in Victoria and Waterloo stations, and even at Tooting for a while.

Lucy Glide

Lucy Glide, born in 1907, lives in Peckham. She was a music hall fan and still enjoys watching musicals on television.

We had silent films at the little cinema at Herne Hill, the Grand, where we used to go for a penny a time.

Was there a pianist there?

We had the pianist for the first film. It was funny to hear them, the galloping [sound effect] and the piano going - it was really great to listen to. But, for the main film, we had a violinist and a little orchestra for the music. First of all, they

had just formes in the front row and being silent films we used to have a laugh - you didn't have to listen to sound, you just had to read. We'd say, "Come on, let's shove the formes over."

It got quite rowdy?

But it was all done in good fun.

Do you recall the Palladium in Brixton?

From what I can remember of it, it was along the Town Hall Parade, opposite the big church there. We never went to that one very often. We used to call that the posh cinema. The seats were a bit dearer. And on the other corner where

"The posh cinema": Palladium Brixton (c1913)

"The fleapit": Brixton Pavilion (c1911)

"You thought you were sitting in the open air": the Astoria Brixton (1929 photograph)

the Tate Library was, there was the Pavilion. We used to call that the fleapit.

That's still there, as the Ritzy.

It is. It wasn't very nice, we didn't like it very much in there. I only went once or twice there, because where you sat, if it was rainy, you had a shower on top of you - it had a leaky roof and everything. Between the Pavilion and the Tate Library, we had the Brixton Theatre. The entrance was next to the Library, but it lay at the back of the Library. We saw

ballet there, and we saw Anton Dolin and Alicia Markova there. Then we had the music hall opposite, the Empress. That was a lovely place.

Did you go a lot to that?

Yes. We used to go every Monday night. We used to walk to Brixton from where we lived and walk home again. Sixpence up in the gods - that was all we could afford. We saw some beautiful shows in that place. We had Gracie Fields there. Donald Peers. The Sherry Brothers with, they called it, the Sherry Cocktail - there were four sisters and five brothers and they used to put on a marvellous show. And then we had Jack Hylton's band play there. We had Billy Cotton there. All the bands I've mentioned we had at the Empress as well as the Astoria. And we had real entertainment, but we don't get none of that now.

How did you know which films were on? Did you read it in the paper?

No, they used to advertise mostly in the streets. You didn't have the pages in the paper, not like you have now. They never told you, you just saw bill stickers. They used to put them up, where they were taking place, and we used to take our pick from that.

Did you buy film magazines?

Film magazines, and they used to have these glossy postcards of different film stars. There was a shop near where I worked in Charing Cross Road where they used to sell all these glossy photographs and we used to get stacks of them.

Did you ever go to films up the West End?

One place we went to - that was the Tivoli in the Strand. It was a lovely place. Sometimes when we finished work, we used to work our money out and, if we could afford it, we used to go. At the Tivoli we saw *Rio Rita* with Bebe Daniels and the first *Showboat* - that was Allan Jones and Irene Dunne. The Alhambra - that was a music hall but that turned into a cinema in the finish and we saw Paul Whiteman in a film there, more like a revue film, and John Boles was in it and Bing Crosby.

When you were courting, did you go the cinema?

Yes. The Trocadero, at the Elephant. But we used to go all over the place, really - wherever the best films were.

What do you remember about the Trocadero?

It was more Gothic style. It looked like a church inside, and that Astoria at Streatham, that looked like a church inside, Egyptian style, but the one at Brixton was the best one of the two. The Brixton Astoria, that was beautiful in there. The ceiling, you thought you were sitting in the open air at night time. The ceiling was midnight blue and it had all stars in it. And there was a sort of gallery, in Italian style, with all grapevines. It was a marvellous place. When we first went there we all looked up and it was really wonderful, a cinema to be like that.

What were the programmes like?

We had the main film and then we had a feature film and then we had a comedy and then we had a newsreel film and that lasted ten minutes to half-an-hour - and then a band show on the stage.

Good value. It's a good evening out.

It was for a shilling. The people who paid for the dearer seats had the advantage of the long distance seeing it from the back, but I think we had the best of both worlds down in front because we could see everything that went on there.

Leslie Wilkinson

Leslie Wilkinson, born in 1909, worked for various film magazines, still lives in Streatham, and remains a fan of silent films at the National Film Theatre.

We came to Streatham when I was about four or five in 1913. My father had the first shop in Wellfield Road, opposite a pub called the Leigham Arms. He was there for twenty-three years. We used to advertise the two Streatham cinemas, which were the Golden Domes and the Streatham Empire. The Golden Domes was near where the General Post Office is now in Streatham High Road. The Streatham Empire was down what they call the Dip, just past the Bedford Park Pub,

nearly opposite the big Safeways there. People came into the shop and there was this bill that stuck out a mile that was the Empire, and the Golden Domes was on the other side. And naturally we got free tickets, so I grew up going at least twice a week to the pictures.

Did your parents take you?

My mother used the tickets and told me I used to crawl under the seats at that age. It was very nice in the cinema then because the attendants would bring around tea, all thrown in with it. In the war years, at the school I used to go to, Wednesday afternoon was free to watch football matches, which I didn't go to. I used to go to the pictures, my mother and I. And from the Streatham Empire, we used to go across the road to what was called a national restaurant - it was just below that big Safeways in Streatham - and then we'd take the tram or bus and go down to the Mitcham Lane Picture Palace the same evening.

The Mitcham Lane Picture Palace was a rather cheap little old cinema but very interesting - they used to have all of the old serials, people like Ruth Roland and Pearl White. On Saturday afternoon they had what they used to call penny pictures: kids were allowed in for a penny and, whereas the full programme was two hours and a half in the evening, they used to give the kids two hours of that same programme and usually lop off the opening of the big picture so as to fit it in. They might start on reel 4 to get the rest of the programme in - which was usually a serial episode and a couple of comedies for the children. The Mitcham Lane had a balcony where the kids used to misbehave on a Saturday afternoon. It sounds awful but they used to spit over the top onto the kids below. Somebody used to come round with a squeegy disinfectant thing they'd pump onto the kids...

At the Streatham Golden Domes, the manager was a chap called Robert Chambers, but the boss really was his mother, Mrs. Chambers. She always seemed to have charge of the finances and could be seen going to the bank on Monday morning. And he ran a club just across the road in Streatham.

And the Streatham Empire, the manager there was Gordon Porter, and he used to stand outside the cinema in evening dress and all that...

Golden Domes Streatham c1914

And greet the patrons. Did all the cinemas have commissionaires or just the very big ones?

I think, the very big ones. The fellow who used to come and paste the bills up for us, from the Streatham Empire, was a young chap, but he often used to appear as a commissionaire in a uniform - Jack was his name.

At the Golden Domes, was there a piano or a small orchestra?

They had a small orchestra, a very good orchestra. They had about seven people in the orchestra which played for the big picture, half the programme. The second feature just had ordinary piano accompaniment.

What about the other cinemas?

The Mitcham Lane one had a trio. The Streatham Empire had a ladies orchestra - Katherine Fryer and the Grey Ladies Orchestra - and she used to give a violin

Empire Streatham in 1912

solo. She led the orchestra and again they played for the big picture and perhaps some other quarter of an hour, and piano accompaniment for the rest of the programme. We used to follow Pearl White at the Golden Domes. She was in a whole series of things - she was in *The Exploits of Elaine, The Perils of Pauline, The Fatal Ring, The Lightning Raider, Pearl of the Army,* which was the end of the First World War. Another serial I always remember was *Patria,* which starred Mrs. Vernon Castle - she was a famous dancer, and her husband, Vernon Castle, was killed in the war.

During the First World War, do you remember any newsreels?

Topical Budget was the one at the Golden Domes and the Streatham Empire had a different one, I can't remember what that was. There was a Pathe Pictorial - that had things of interest. But I was more interested in the dramas, heavy dramas.

When you were small, did you find it heavy-going to watch a full-length feature film plus...?

No, no. My great favourite - I was eight or nine at the time - was Theda Bara, the vamp. And I followed the serials. Then in about 1929 the Streatham Astoria turned up, where the Odeon is now. And that rather put a damper on the old Golden Domes. Golden Domes still had the contract to show MGM films but people flocked to something new. After that, the Empire closed.

Once the Streatham Astoria opened and the Gaumont and the Regal, Streatham had a very good choice of big cinemas. Somehow I never took to the Streatham Astoria.

Can you say something about cinemas at the beginning of the War?

When the War started, all cinemas had to close by half-past seven to eight o'clock in the evening. They anticipated raids. But, actually, it didn't last very long. They soon went back, because that was what they called the Phoney War. But I remember going to the Gaumont Streatham and the film

Pearl White in The Lightning Raider *(1918) with Warner Oland and Henry G. Sell*

was *Jesse James* with Tyrone Power, and it was the first time they had to have the lights out early in the evening. When we went to the cinema it was all right but when we came out I was surprised - it was all dark.

Did they give air raid warnings in cinemas for people to leave?

Yes, but often people stayed put.

So you stayed, did you?

It happened. It wasn't a cinema. The Penge Empire. I used to go there - they had a very good repertory company, Harry Henson's Court Players. And this was that September night when they bombed the docks. We were caught and they advised us not to go out and we were in that theatre all night.

So what did you do all night?

The two pianists who accompanied them, they kept playing. We sat in the stalls. And daylight came and the raid was over. We went up onto the roof, looked across. That was a very bad blitz.

Leslie and Peggy Smith in the former restaurant of the Astoria Streatham, now the Odeon, where only the original ceiling remains

Leslie and Peggy Smith

Leslie and Peggy Smith, born in 1911 and 1914 respectively, recall the cinemas of Streatham and Tooting. Leslie, a retired musician, and Peggy still live in South London.

LS: One of the great things of the cinema days was the queueing. Many times we queued and it was pouring with rain, and the owners of the cinema built a kind of glass canopy which people used to queue under. There would be a multiple queue for, shall we say, the shillings and one-and-nines.

PS: And they used to call out "Twelve at two shillings-and-threepence". And you'd think, "I've stood here long enough" and you would rush in. And they used to do that to sell the [more expensive] seats. The atmosphere was always the same inside the cinema. We were bored to tears with the adverts and the Pathe News roaring out and you would hear the curtains close with a rattle, then it all became quiet and the main film came on. Everybody was chatting like mad until the film came on. Then it was all hush.

The restaurant area as it was in 1930 with Egyptian-style columns and Lloyd Loom wicker chairs

If you went with a young man, you expected him to pay?

PS: Yes, I never paid for myself. That was a waste of time.

What are your memories of the Streatham Astoria?

LS: The Streatham Astoria was the start of what were called the super cinemas. It was built in the form of an Egyptian temple and all the motifs inside were Egyptian - all the scarabs, the columns, and the capitals on the columns to look like palm trees. It was a very, very beautiful cinema - a fantastic cinema.

Did it have a restaurant?

LS: It had a most beautiful restaurant. Upstairs.

Was that in the same style?

LS: All in the same style, all in the Egyptian style. And that was one of the first instances where people saw what became very popular in those days - Lloyd Loom furniture. The wicker furniture with the glass-top tables and under the glass tops were paper doilies.

PS: No serve yourself. Waitress service.

LS: Waitress service beautifully done. Pots of tea - you didn't have your tea in mugs which you held in two hands.

PS: Muffins in muffin dishes.

LS: And crumpets and tea cakes and cream cakes. It was quite the place to go on Saturday morning, by the way. Because Streatham was one of those very, very polite places. Saturday morning was sports jacket and flannels and "I'm just going down to change the library books, dear. And I'll probably stop for a coffee at the Astoria."

1944 advertisement for the Astoria restaurants, including Streatham

Did people eat in the cinema auditorium?

PS: They used to eat oranges and peanuts in the cheap seats right at the front. We used to turn our noses up at people when they used to eat oranges.

Can you tell me about the Granada in Tooting?

LS: Yes. I remember the Granada being built. And the opening day of the Granada was quite a thing - the whole of Tooting was there to see it. That was built in the form of the Alcazar in Spain and the inside of the Granada was a colour scheme of ochre and gold. It was a huge theatre. There was a very famous organist there and he was also a very fine pianist. I can see now the mighty Wurlitzer rising up out of what would be the equivalent of a theatre pit. And one of the first stage bands I saw there was Geraldo, whose name was Gerald Bright, incidentally - he came from Liverpool. That was Geraldo and his Gaucho Tango Orchestra.

Granada Tooting in 1931

grand way, you went up into the restaurant and ordered coffee or tea or whatever it was, and "Oh, I'll go and get the tickets." And you went to see the box office and got your tickets and you came back and, having had your tea, you went into the auditorium, in a very grand manner. Today there is no sense of occasion in anything. But when you went to the cinema in those days, it was an occasion. You'd arrange to meet her outside the cinema, you'd be looking at your watch, she's late, you're thinking she's not going to come, and then, of course, five minutes later - they're always five minutes late - she arrives. It was an occasion, the coming out and having a coffee somewhere. But there's no sense of occasion today.

PS: In dreadful satin blouses.

LS: At the time he had the tango band at the Savoy and, like a lot of these orchestra leaders who had a resident job, he also went on tour and he toured the Granada circuit. I can see it now: this huge orchestra on stage, all in this theatrical gaucho costume, with the boots, the sash, all satin, all white, and the big sleeves and the great floppy trousers. They were what musicians used to refer to in those days as Whitechapel gauchos. The livery for the staff was blue and red and the Granada at Tooting was famous for its doormen. They had hundreds of people apply for this job as doorman, two doormen, and these two men who were finally picked were both over six feet tall. And I think one was an ex-marine warrant officer and he was known to everyone in the area as "Tiny". He was enormous, this man. There was lots of things written about him, about the special tailor they had to go to, to cut his greatcoat and have his uniform made. It was all publicity.

That also had a very nice restaurant. Nearly all these cinemas had a restaurant, the idea being that when you came out from the film you stopped for a while and had coffee or whatever before going home or even before going in. You might arrange to meet your girlfriend, or the girl would meet her boyfriend - "All right, I'll see you up in the restaurant", instead of waiting out in the street. And if you did it in a

Harold Ramsay at the mighty Wurlitzer of the Granada Tooting

Bill Halle in front of a set of Sous les Toits de Paris at the Museum of the Moving Image

Bill Halle

Bill Halle, born in 1912, became a professional artist. He now lives in South London but recalls cinema-going in places far removed.

I wasn't allowed to go to a cinema until I was six and we were firmly established at Broadstairs and I remember that little cinema at the end of the arcade. When I went in at six, my mother used to wear a very wide-brimmed hat and if anything unsuitable for me came up she would pretend to drop something and bend over me so every film I saw then was censored. I never realised until much later what she was doing. We were living at Harrow when *The Kid* came out, and an uncle who didn't despise the cinema was bowled over by

Charlie Chaplin in The Kid (1921) with Jackie Coogan

Charlie Chaplin in *The Kid* and that someone should make a film in which there wasn't a youthful romance going on, there was just him and this kid. I remember he practically forced me to go, and I hardly understood it then. I was about eight, and that was at the Coliseum Cinema in South Harrow. It was almost like a landmark - people would say "You go past the Coliseum", which they can't do any more.

When did you move to Manchester?

I was about eleven then. We were real cinema addicts by then. Our favourite one there was the Piccadilly Picture Theatre in Piccadilly. It was a lovely cinema - it was one of those cinemas which was wider than it was long, so wherever you sat you had a pretty good seat. It seemed to me to have a very large screen and they were beginning to project much better then. In the early days, films kept breaking down. But at the Piccadilly I never remember it breaking. And we saw films like Lon Chaney in *He Who Gets Slapped,* which was almost an art film. And *Warning Shadows,* which was a German film. They were beginning to show German films.

And they just came to the ordinary cinemas?

Yes. *Metropolis* was at the Regent in Regent Street, Glasgow. Nobody thought of having art cinemas then.

When you lived in Glasgow, did you live near the centre of the city?

Near enough to go in. But there were so many cinemas about that wherever you lived there was a cinema on the next corner. We lived in a district called Crosshill, and there was the Crosshill Cinema there, a rather tatty little place. And then there was a big one called, funnily enough, the B.B. Cinerama - a great big thing like a factory, a horrible place really. I didn't like the look of it as a cinema. We used to go there because it was cheap. And there was one cinema in Glasgow that had settees instead of seats and you were brought tea by waitresses - in fact, they rather went in for that. You know Glasgow goes in for high teas, lots of scones of all descriptions. You could have tea - the sort of restaurant attached to the cinema, that was open to the cinema. You could just go and have tea or have a waitress bring you a tea tray.

"Like a factory": the B.B. Cinerama at Crosshill seen c1946 (later known as the Odeon Eglington Toll)

And this was during the film?

Yes, and I've never seen that anywhere else, even in London.

Where did you move to from Glasgow?

We went to the far north of Scotland. This was a fishing village called Broura, on the east coast of the far north, where they brought round these travelling cinemas. They used to take a hall and the projector, the dynamo thing was on a lorry outside, and they used to show the films in this church hall. It was pretty rough and ready - you sat on hard formes. Somebody local played the piano - rather badly, but good enough. They would come for about three weeks and show about three or four films, and then you wouldn't see them again for a long time - they'd gone on to other villages. It was rather lonely up there - a small village, and we were English and didn't know anyone. There was my sister and her Scottish husband and me and an Alsatian dog, and the evenings did hang rather heavy there, especially the winter ones, so it was nice to know the cinema was coming.

And then we moved to Wick - that's a fishing market town - and they had a most enterprising cinema there. They showed a lot of German films. The audience seemed quite enthusiastic - the Scots have an intellectual streak in them somewhere. I saw Garbo's second film, *The Temptress*, and I was determined to see her next film whatever happened. But, unfortunately, we moved then to this village in the far north of Scotland and then over to Wick, and *Flesh and the Devil* was shown in Glasgow. And in those days once films were

Garbo with John Gilbert in Flesh and the Devil *(1926)*

shown in the centre of town and then round the suburbs, they just completely disappeared - you couldn't get them back again. I asked the Wick manager if he would show the film, and I had such a nice letter back - we will show it but it will take a little time. And just a week before it came, we moved down to London, so I never saw it until they showed it at the Dominion recently.

I must tell you about a cinema at Whitstable, which is now a supermarket. At Whitstable, they had breaks - you had to wait sometimes ten minutes while they threaded the next reel in, and there was a lot of stamping of feet and coughing - everybody coughed. That was where the manager always appeared in evening dress and shook hands with everyone. We always went to the balcony. You went up to the booking office and the tickets, instead of being paper ones, were brass plates, quite heavy, and you took these brass plates down the side of the cinema, down an alleyway at the side of the cinema and there was a door there which led up to the balcony - I'm sure, up wooden stairs. There was someone standing at the top to take the brass plates. They just used the same brass plates over and over. And a thing that intrigued me: I noticed, when you were up in the balcony, the screen was where the street was - at the front rather than at the back of the cinema.

Did you always sit in the balcony?

The stalls were considered terrible. You heard the crackling of bags of peanuts and stuff, and yells and shouts. One was safely above all that.

Did you eat in the cinema?

No, we never did. Never.

I'd imagine people cracking these monkey nuts must have been rather distracting?

Terrible. One did anything to get away. The stalls were sixpence and ninepence, and the balcony was one shilling-and-threepence. Although we were very hard up at that time, Mother insisted on the balcony. She said she couldn't stand those people down below.

Bertha Downes

Bertha Downes, born in 1912, recalls her childhood in Westminster where she helped her father bring up her ten brothers and sisters. In 1931 the family moved over the bridge to Lambeth where she spent her married life. She now lives at the Oval.

Do you have early memories of the cinema in Westminster, when you were small?

Yes, I used to go with my older brothers to Strutton Ground, Saturday mornings. It was a market place and it used to be a penny to see all the cowboy things and "look behind you, guv'nor!" attitude, Pearl White on the railway, things like that. There was a lady who used to play the piano there. It was absolute chaos. The kids were all shouting out and throwing peanuts. In later years, I was able to go to the Biograph in Wilton Road, but I was by then quite grown up. That was much more select, much quieter.

The first time I ever went anywhere really big on my own I was eighteen, I was with my girlfriend. And I went to the Metropole on their opening night and I was out till twelve o'clock that night. I'm sure the film I saw was *Jenny Lind* - the "Swedish nightingale". There was no royalty, no big show of red carpets, or anything like that. It was just everybody going because it was a new cinema.

Did your brothers go to the cinema a lot?

They were grown-ups after the War, the three brothers older than myself. They would go over the bridge - Westminster Bridge - and there was the Gatti's. That was a fleapit. And that used to be threepence. And I said to one of my brothers one day, "Can't I come with you?" "No, you can't." I was then about fourteen or fifteen. They would

"The best bob's worth in South London": the Trocadero Elephant and Castle

never take their sister to somewhere like that. You see, the Gatti's was the kind of place where all the lads would meet and they could have a laugh or a lark, where they could shout out, "Look behind you, guv'nor!", "Mind, he's got you!", "Punch him!", "Hit him hard!"

No, I never went there but I did go across the road to the Canterbury. That was more a family place. Mum would go in the afternoon for threepence, take the baby and a bottle of milk for the baby.

By the time I was seventeen or eighteen, my mother had died and I was head cook and bottle washer in the house, looking after the younger ones. So I didn't have the kind of get-about teenage life really. I could never go very regularly to the Canterbury. But when I met my husband, that was quite different because by then I didn't have quite such a heavy responsibility - my brothers and sisters were getting a bit older. I could leave them and go to the pictures.

And that was your main form of entertainment when you went out together?

We used to go to the cinema once a week on a Thursday to the Trocadero at the Elephant and Castle. The best bob's worth in South London. It was only a shilling to go there. It was a big place, a big oval fronted place. I used to take my brothers and sisters, the younger ones. The kids on the top were dreadful. Still shouting, still calling out.

When you went in the evening time with your young man, you all wanted a seat at the back. You didn't want to be at the front where they were all shouting and things were coming over the top. You got the main film and another film and a comedy and then you got the British Movietone News and there was always three music hall turns. And that was a wonderful programme. It was big and it wasn't the rough house for the teenagers - you couldn't go in there in a gang and have a fight because the man on the door would stop you. It was then becoming a rather sophisticated, proper place for adults. When Mum and Dad would want to go out, perhaps Saturday night, it would be on the level like you would be going now to the theatre in the West End.

Why did you go on Thursdays?

At the time I met my young man he was unemployed and he used to get the dole money on Thursdays.

Did you have to queue at the Trocadero?

You always had to queue. And you always went out of the house ten or fifteen minutes earlier because you knew you would have to queue. And when you got there and the queue was a mile long, you'd say, "Oh, we'll never get in here." And very often that was it. You'd got there too late to queue. You just got chopped or you were lucky and you would go in.

Did your husband-to-be always pay for you?

Oh yes. He took you out and that was it - not like today, shares or Dutch treats. He bought you sweets as well. Bitter almonds. You never see them in the shops any more. They're

"A sleazy kind of look": Robert Mitchum in Macao (1952)

small, dark chocolate and nuts. And he used to buy me Neapolitan chocolates or Milk Tray toffee.

And did you read about films? Did you buy Picturegoer?

No, I could never afford that.

The Warsaw Concerto was played in Dangerous Moonlight *(1941) which starred Sally Gray and Anton Walbrook*

Did you have any favourite stars?

Oh yeah, did I? Sounds a bit silly now. My children have a go at me. "Robert Mitchum's on tonight, Mum." I've watched all his films without perhaps remembering some of the names. I watch all his films, old or not. He's the one I never miss. He still does it: he'll stand in a doorway, sleazy kind of look, very compelling eyes. You know, you've seen him. He just comes in and stands there, never smiles. The lazy lackadaisical way of saying things, you read his face.

Did you go to the cinema once you were married?

Once the baby was born we didn't go together to the pictures. Johnny was about two years when the War came. That was it. No more cinema, no more nothing. I used to go to the cinema when I was evacuated - that was to Henley-on-Thames. Quite a nice area, quite different. But there were lots and lots of London people there. London people from the East End when the docks were bombed, they all came down - so you weren't really a fly in a big jar of ointment. We all used to go to the pictures there. One particular film from the wartime I remember...when the Warsaw Concerto was being played [*Dangerous Moonlight*].

Why does that stick in your memory?

It was a Saturday evening and there were a whole lot of us there together as friends. And the place was full of soldiers, mostly the Essex regiment - Londoners, you see. And you felt like that [really close].

Sid Cove with his model of the Elephant and Castle Trocadero

Sid Cove

Sid Cove, born in 1917, was a cinema projectionist who became a cabinet maker. He has built an intricate model of a cinema which remains a prize possession in his flat near the Oval. His reminiscences also appear in Working There.

One place I used to go in Peckham High Street, the building's still there - it used to be called Thorn's Hall. It was a little "penny rush". Every Saturday morning for the kids, they used to put on all the old comedy films, all the Charlie Chaplin, Laurel and Hardy, all the little things with the music. You used to go up there with a penny.

One thing we used to do to get our money. In Peckham, about 1930 they demolished a lot of wooden houses. They were all old and dangerous, they were fire hazards, so they started knocking them down. So me and a few of the lads nearby used to go and take timber that we could manage. Bring it home. And we used to get in one of our gardens and spend all our nights out of school in the evening chopping it up. We used to get the firewood all ready and stock it in one of our sheds in the garden, and Saturday morning we used to go out selling it. We used to give a bowl of firewood for a penny or tuppence, because everybody used to light their own fire then. You had coal fires. You'd light them with wood and paper. Anyway, they used to like to buy off the kids because

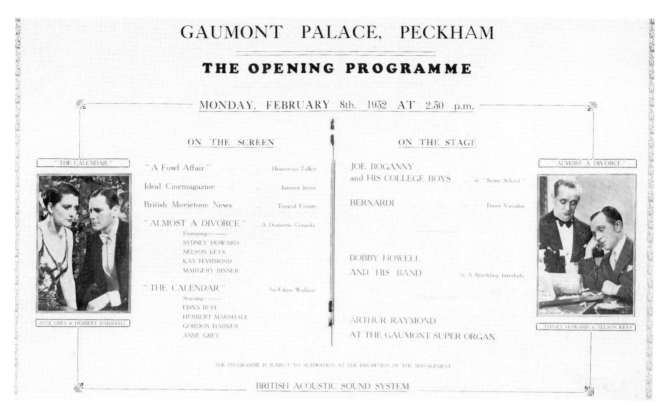

GAUMONT PALACE, PECKHAM

THE OPENING PROGRAMME

MONDAY, FEBRUARY 8th, 1932 AT 2.30 p.m.

ON THE SCREEN		ON THE STAGE	
"A Fowl Affair"	Humorous Talkie	JOE BOGANNY and HIS COLLEGE BOYS	in "Some School"
Ideal Cinemagazine	Interest Items		
British Movietone News	Topical Events	BERNARDI	Tenor Vocalist
"ALMOST A DIVORCE"	A Domestic Comedy		
Featuring— SYDNEY HOWARD NELSON KEYS KAY HAMMOND MARGERY BINNER		BOBBY HOWELL AND HIS BAND	in A Sparkling Interlude
"THE CALENDAR"	by Edgar Wallace		
Starring— EDNA BEST HERBERT MARSHALL GORDON HARKER ANNE GREY		ARTHUR RAYMOND AT THE GAUMONT SUPER ORGAN	

THE PROGRAMME IS SUBJECT TO ALTERATION AT THE DISCRETION OF THE MANAGEMENT

BRITISH ACOUSTIC SOUND SYSTEM

we gave them about ten sticks and that was their whack. But with us kids, we pick it all for nothing, we chop it up all for nothing, we give them a great big heap, they got a good two-penny-worth of firewood. The money we got from that goes to the pies and mash shop - we got one in Peckham called Mansies. That was our little treat. We used to go up there about dinner time when we sold our wood, into the pie and mash shop, and then to Thorn's to see the films. Because you didn't get much. We'd get a farthing. You could buy things for a farthing - you could get a Spanish licorice.

And a visit to the cinema was good value.

Look at this programme [*in opening brochure of the Gaumont Palace Peckham*]: you've got two films, a newsreel, a cartoon and interest films, you've got two acts, Joe and his College Boys, and you've got an orchestra, and then you've got the organ show. That was quite a show. And in the winter, when it's cold, you're in a warm building and it's a place for meeting your friends. And you were well behaved. You'd go in there and sit there and you're a stranger to me and you can sit next to me for three hours and nobody interferes with you. There's no mucking about. Everybody's come to see the film. If you're a teenager you have a chat with each other, but normally my mother and father used to go, all the locals used to go and sit there and enjoy a film. We were quite a family. There were six or seven of us. My mother used to go there and halfway through she's away.

A good place to relax?

That's it. The kids are happy and the heat and darkness, it sends you off, because my mother used to work late at nights, on the machine work, making stuff. The van used to drop a lot of dresses off, all cut, and she used to have to sew them together. That's how she kept the family. Your dad was invariably out of work because pre-war there was great unemployment in this country.

Was your dad unemployed?

My dad worked, but he worked for the Council, what they call casual work. And hundreds did the same. You'd report every morning at the office and they'd say, "You - you - you - you." And they'd go round or call your names out, "You go down there and work". And he might be working on the roads, in the offices. And twenty come home, no work. Twenty work and twenty home, and that was what it was all about.

"Out of this world": King Kong (1933)

Did your dad ever take you when you were children?

I can honestly say I never been to the pictures with my dad. My mum loved it but my dad'd sooner have a drink. My dad'd sooner have a pint. To go into a pub, it didn't interest me. Working in the cinema, I was tied up. My day was full from early in the morning until late at night.

But your mum was happy to take you to the pictures.

My mum, yes. My mum and me, we would queue up - whenever you went to the pictures you'd always expect to get in a queue, you never expected to go straight in. You knew your programmes - that was another thing in those days.

Half-past three was a change of house, half-past seven was another change of house. We go now, we won't get in, so we go at about half-past, get in the queue. And what happens in the queue is that you've got the old bloke selling peanuts. You spend your time eating peanuts and all that outside in the queue, so you can see marks along the outside of the cinema where people had been queueing, with all the grease. It was a regular thing. Everybody queued up.

Did it turn you into a film fan?

Yes. In those days all the children went to the cinemas, as you've got television today. Then it was the cinema. My brother, he sometimes used to go three times a day. He used to go when it opened at midday, pop home, have something to eat, go to another one, and perhaps on my day off I'd go of a night-time with him. So three trips a day, because it might be an occasion where you got three films out and they were all ones you mustn't miss. Although it did happen they all came back again on a Sunday release. Some cinemas used to run a week, and some used to run Monday, Tuesday and Wednesday, change Thursday, Friday and Saturday, and then they'd change again on the Sunday, just for Sunday.

Which were the films that you liked best?

King Kong was good. It was something out of this world in that day and age. And they had a great big display of an ape climbing a skyscraper. It was really good. When they had big films they always used to put on a big display. They all used to advertise their films in expensive billboarding of some type. Now *Rome Express*, they had a big train, all decorated round the front. And *Tarzan, The Apeman*. There used to be a chap who worked all Saturday evening to erect advertising for the coming film. There were quite a few displays. *King Kong* was a good one. Tarzan - as youngsters we used to like that, it was all the rage. That's why they kept making them.

Vi Turner and Fred Creasey outside the former Regal Camberwell, now a Mecca bingo hall

Vi Turner and Fred Creasey

Vi Turner, born in 1919, and her brother Fred Creasey, born in 1931, recall their early cinema-going experiences together. Vi still lives in South London but Fred has re-located to the Isle of Dogs.

Vi, when you were a little girl, were you taken to the cinema?

VT: We were taken to the music hall more than the cinema but when I was about five or six I used to go to the cinema every single week, never missed. My big brother used to take me.

Which cinemas did you go to?

VT: Mostly it was the Brixton Astoria because that had just opened. I remember it being built and I remember it opening. We used to go every Sunday and it was a shilling to go in. I saw my very first talkie there. It was called *Blackmail*.

The auditorium of the Brixton Astoria was done like a balcony on a Spanish house. The ceiling was a dome and it was like the sky and it had stars in it. And they used to put up on the screen: "This cinema is perfumed with Yardley's Lavender". And you used to sniff - "Doesn't this smell lovely!"

I remember seeing *Dracula* there and, I don't know if it was in the middle or the interval, somebody came out onto this little balcony dressed as Dracula and they shone the spotlight onto him and everybody screamed. It really frightened you because it was so unexpected.

Actually, we used to go to the Brixton Astoria so much we used to get a little magazine sent to us. And it told you the films on for that month, and it had all the Astorias - Brixton Astoria, Streatham Astoria - and I remember there was a great big picture of somebody, the boss of Paramount - was it Gulliver? - on the front of it. And we used to get that sent every month, through the door.

Fred, how old were you when you first got taken to the pictures?

FC: I must have been taken to the cinema when I was very young and I remember being quite frightened. I don't know what I saw but I do remember being quite scared and I didn't want to go for a long time. But then kids at school talked about films. I remember the first film I ever saw which I really loved and gave me the taste for going back to the cinema and that was *The Adventures of Robin Hood*. It was a colour film with Errol Flynn. I remember living that film afterwards, making wooden swords and bows and arrows and all that kind of thing.

Brixton Astoria in 1929

What other cinemas did you go to?

VT: There was a big one called the Trocadero and it was really great value for money. You used to get two full-length films and about an hour's stage show.

FC: Teddy Joyce and his Orchestra in the interval.

VT: And Quentin Maclean playing the organ.

FC: You must have been in the cinema for about four hours in those days.

VT: I remember once I went with a friend to the Trocadero. We walked home from the Elephant down

Walworth Road, because we lived at Camberwell then, and we got in at midnight. It shows you how long the films were on.

Did you not feel nervous going round the streets?

VT: It's funny - I never really thought about it. We used to go and get a penneth of chips about half-past ten at night at the fish and chip shop. You couldn't send your kids to do that now.

Most of the big cinemas had a variety show as well?

VT: That's right. I remember seeing Ted Ray at the Astoria. *Fiddling and Fooling* it was called. He was between the films.

Advertisement for the three South London Astorias for May 1943

FC: You just wandered into films. You didn't wait for the beginning. And you sat around to where you came in.

VT: You could go into the cinema any time.

FC: Except for the big films like *Gone with the Wind* where you had to queue up and they only let you in when the film started. I seem to remember even in some of the local cinemas they had booking for *Gone with the Wind*.

One of the things I remember when I was a kid was hanging around cinemas and asking someone to take you in. If it was an "A", you'd say, "Can you take me in, mister?"

Did your mother know?

FC: No. Mothers would go barmy if they thought their kids were hanging around cinemas.

VT: You couldn't do that at all now. It's a different world altogether to what it was then.

Did you have a favourite star?

FC: I'll tell you who I remember you talking about when I was a kid: George Raft.

VT: That's who my favourite was.

FC: What was that film he danced a tango?

VT: *Bolero*, with Carole Lombard. And that's the first time I heard that music, and I saw it about six times. My mum used to say, "I'm fed up of dusting George Raft's photo." I had photos everywhere.

Where did you get the photos?

VT: Some magazines you used to get a free photo. Picturegoer, it was called. And Woolworth's used to sell film star pictures. They were about threepence each, and they used to sell loads, of all film stars.

Frank was mad on Bing Crosby. We saw all his films, bought all his records - half-a-crown Brunswick records. And my friend, she was mad on Bing Crosby - we didn't have much money in those days and she used to get a half-a-crown Brunswick record of Bing singing and she had to give her dad sixpence a week to pay for it.

FC: I certainly remember going through this little craze of sending off for pictures. Funnily, they were all British ones I had - Margaret Lockwood, Phyllis Calvert...and particularly, I remember, I was in love with Jean Simmons. She had a very small part in *The Way to the Stars* - she sings a song in it - and I had a signed photograph of her in that role.

Did everybody talk about films a lot in the Thirties and Forties?

VT: Because they didn't have any other form of entertainment. There was just the radio. I remember talking over the wall and the girls next door: we'd say, "Oh, we went

Jean Simmons in The Way to the Stars *(1945)*

to see a lovely film...", and we used to sit on the wall and tell them all the story of it.

What about the war time? Did you go to the cinema?

VT: At the beginning of the War nothing happened. They called it the Phoney War. We thought directly war was declared we were really going to be bombed and blasted out of our homes - and nothing happened. And about a year later, when we were in the pictures, that's the night it really started.

And if something happened when you were in the cinema, they'd put a slide up on the screen?

VT: Yes, usually saying "Air raid in progress - you may leave the cinema if you so desire." But you hardly ever used to bother. We still went to the pictures in spite of the bombing.

FC: Yes. Got you away from it all, I suppose.

VT: It was funny - if it was gone six o'clock and the air raid warning hadn't gone, you'd say, "They're late tonight." What was that cinema we went to when the air raid started on the docks?

FC: That was the Regal in Walworth Road - Camberwell, we called it. Walworth Road
becomes
Camberwell Road
and it was just about
Camberwell.

VT: That was
pretty new then.
And we saw My Son,
My Son with Louis
Hayward. They put
up on the screen
"There is an air raid
in progress" when we
came out.

The Regal, near Walworth Road, Camberwell circa 1946

FC: It must have been the beginning of the Blitz proper.

VT: And when we came out, all the docks were on fire. It looked as if the whole of the world was on fire. And we walked home.

FC: And halfway we stopped in one of those brick shelters.

VT: It got a little nearer, so we bunked into this shelter.

FC: I thought it was funny in retrospect - I didn't think it was funny at the time - that they were still making films about the First World War, because My Son, My Son was one of those stories about a son who's a bit of a so-and-so but makes good in the end by capturing a machine-gun post in the First World War. So the last bit of the film was Louis Hayward creeping across no man's land with all these bangs and things going on, and there were actually real bangs outside.

Louis Hayward (right) with Brian Aherne in My Son, My Son

VT: And a real air raid on.

There were some cinemas that were hit.

VT: The Regal in Walworth Road: I had a friend killed there. It was a chap, they were watching a film, and it got a direct hit. Do you remember the Purple? It got bombed and the very film they were showing was *So This Is London*. I remember seeing the big poster outside saying *So This Is London*.

FC: The whole cinema was gutted but they managed to leave this poster. It was a comedy with Robertson Hare. That must have been at night when nobody was in it.

Len England outside the former Gaumont Streatham

Len England

———————— *Len England, born in 1920,
has retired to Wales after a
career in market research.
He was part of Mass
Observation's well-known,
large-scale investigation of
everyday life in the Thirties
and Forties and became a
director of that organisation
after the War. He also
appears in Film Talk.*

I was born and bred in Streatham Hill, very close to the
Theatre. My father was a secretary of a big wood firm. My
mother was an ex-teacher. I was an only child, so cinema-

going was much of an occasion, when I used to go often with
my mother, particularly to the Astoria. My clear memory of
that, in those days, you had an A picture, a B picture, and
organ, a Pathe Gazette, probably a short, and forthcoming
attractions. And you used to go in whenever you felt like it,
although there was an alleyway where people would wait or
queue until the cinema was empty - it seems unbelievable but
it was often full. I remember tea was part of the ceremonial
occasion of going to the cinema in the upstairs lounge of the
Astoria. And you used to have things like roe on toast for tea
or toasted buns, but there was always something special about
it. And my mother and I used to watch who was going in and
that was part of the occasion, watching.

The cinemas in Streatham are clearly in my mind. There
were two old fleapits which were the start of my cinema
career. One was the Golden Domes, which had two beautiful

The Astoria Streatham in 1930

painted golden domes outside it and which was in the middle of Streatham, fairly close to being opposite what was the Astoria later on. And the other one was the Streatham Empire which was turned into a cinema from being a dance hall or old theatre or something, by Streatham Station where the trams turned round. That didn't last very long after my memories start but the Golden Domes did and I have clear recollections of sitting at the back of the stalls with my mother listening to the bangs at the end of *King of the Khyber Rifles*, which I think was the first talking picture I'd ever seen.

The sort of film my mother loved was the standard good, soppy Hollywood films. She wasn't uncritical. She was a school mistress, but she did like the soppy ones, so the ideal thing were the MGM greats, be it *Romeo and Juliet*, or weepies, Garbo and those sort of things. She went to enjoy herself. She used to say, "Wasn't that nice?" She used to embarrass me like mad by saying when it got exciting, etc. She used to hate being frightened and she wouldn't go and see anything horrific. So I have been trained basically not to like horror films.

My main cinema-going is associated with the three big cinemas in Streatham. First, the Astoria which was built about a year after the Brixton Astoria and was very gaudy. Second, the Gaumont which was built two years later and was even more palatial - colonial facade, etc. And thirdly was the Regal Streatham which I have no recollection of going to until shortly before the war.

Was there a point when you started going to the cinema with friends?

I remember going with a girlfriend whose hand I held in 1938 but I suppose I never went with girlfriends in the standard way. I was fairly narrowly religious in my teens and I went a lot with Crusaders, who were a fairly evangelical lot. They wouldn't object to your going to the cinema but they wouldn't make a point of going in a group.

Did you ever go to a cinema on a Sunday?

I never went on Sunday, ever. I would be going to Evensong, but if not I would have felt that Sunday was a special day. I did go once, though, in the middle of the War, on leave, and felt I was a real devil. I remember clearly going when Dorothy, my future wife, came back on leave with me.

The Gaumont Palace Streatham in 1932 with "colonial facade"

It was the first time I'd ever done it, but we only had a weekend leave and we wanted to be alone there, too. We went to the Odeon Balham.

What was the atmosphere like in cinemas in the Thirties?

It was much more lively. It was much more of an event. The cinemas which were built then, with permanent in going and out going, had usherettes going up and down all the time showing people to their seats. It had ice-cream girls going all the time. It had the mighty Wurlitzer and with occasionally script up to sing along. But certainly in the afternoons the cinema wasn't terribly full. So you got great empty spaces, but you still had this break up with lots of trailers which people loved. I don't think you had advertising shorts but you certainly had other shorts of either the Three Stooges and Laurel and Hardy-type or travel which was rather fun and people at the end would say, "And so we say farewell to sunny Bali", etc. You then had the second feature which lasted 58 minutes and was Charlie Chan or the Falcon or the Saint which were all exactly the same but were really quite good.

I wrote a line about every film that I'd seen right up to about the Fifties. Even when I was in the War, I sent it back to a friend of mine who wasn't in the Army and he had to write up all the films that I'd seen overseas. That was collecting rather than criticising. What surprises me reading this list is the things which I've clean forgotten about and thought were very good at the time like *Mad About Music*. I certainly remember the enormous pleasure of going to see *Snow White and the Seven Dwarfs*. I don't remember which year *Fantasia* came out but that does ring an enormous bell with me still.

George Formby lets Hitler have it in Let George Do It (1940)

How did you get involved with Mass Observation?

I was on one of the panels of Mass Observation when I was at school. They wanted lots of people to record exactly what they were doing with their own opinions because Tom Harrison believed quite rightly that the papers only collected the top upper crust. At the beginning of the War he asked if anyone was interested in helping him do observations - he was trying to check war morale. Mass Observation were pioneers of trying to get at what real people did and thought and felt. Cinema was at the centre of this - it was everywhere, in the back streets and everywhere else. It was the pop culture in those days.

So how did you check morale in the cinemas?

I would watch the newsreels and see if they clapped Churchill and how much, note it down and then I would often leave. But the period when cinema was noisy and reactionary was only about eighteen months, until people settled down to the War. I saw *Let George Do It* about twelve times. There was a great deal of valid information that you could get: there was a dream sequence where George Formby knocked out Hitler and if morale was good everybody laughed, if morale was bad nobody thought it was funny. It was a morale check. After *Let George Do It,* cinemas went calm again, partly because Hitler settled down or whatever it was.

I know you've stopped going regularly to the cinema but do you miss the big screen and being with an audience?

I did go out of my way to see *Gandhi* on the big screen because I knew it would be absolutely hopeless except on the big screen. I don't think I've been to the local cinema in the last two years. But *La Traviata* is an example of something where I would try and get good sound as well as an audience. It was incredible when we saw *La Traviata* in this local cinema. There was just not a sound for about two minutes after the end of the film, and then everybody clapped, which was like going back...it was just like going to an opera. The dead silence at the end of the film I hadn't heard for years. The whole audience couldn't do anything except stunned silence. It was lovely.

Denis Norden

Denis Norden, born in 1922, is the well-known radio and television personality. His reminiscences also appear in Working There and Film Talk.

There was a purpose in picture palaces being palaces. The smell of them was palatial. People went once a week and that was the very least they went - it wasn't unusual for people to go twice a week and very often more than twice a week because, remember, that part of London [around the Elephant and Castle] was very low quality housing, it was a slum area. The back of the Trocadero, from the projection room on a hot night when we opened the door and walked out on the flat roof, we looked down on the Peabody Buildings and they were Dickensian. We had a pair of binoculars because people didn't have curtains and things like that.

So it was a very poor area with all the tensions of that kind of inner city area - tremendous conflict with the police, no mercy shown on either side. And when you came in the cinema you really were getting the only touch of luxury you could possibly acquire in those days. The seats were more

The Elephant and Castle Trocadero

December 1930 advertisement

comfortable, the chairs, cushions were more comfortable than anything at home. The Trocadero was your top class local cinema. For the real birthday treat you went, as they say, "up West" - you went to one of the West End cinemas, where they had to fulfil even higher expectations. So the Empire Leicester Square, before they opened, the ushers used to line up in the foyer and smoke Havana cigars and puff out the smoke, so as to give you that smell which is what you pay for. And the loos, if you saw the loos, even in the suburban cinemas, they were marvellous. "You dreamed you lay in marble halls..." - these were the only marble halls you ever got to, the loos. Jimmy James, a comedian at the time, was taken to the Leicester Square

Odeon or something like that and they said, "What do you think about it?", and he said, "It doesn't half make your willie look shabby."

The kind of social function, there is nothing in today's world which approximates it. It was an outing. People used to take food. Eating was part of going to the cinema. There were oranges, there were apples, there were the peanuts, the unshelled peanuts, not your cissy peanuts that they get today. At the end of the day, when everyone had left, you crunched along the rows to get from one place to another.

I remember I did relief round the [Hyams] circuit at the Troxy Commercial Road, and a famous American performer who did cine-variety came out for the first show - two o'clock it would be in the afternoon, somewhere round about that. And he came off and I happened to be backstage and he said, "I've never seen anything like that" - and there

Kids queueing outside the Elephant and Castle Trocadero

was the whole of the front row sitting sideways on, not sitting facing, sitting sideways on suckling babies. Regardless of what you saw from suckling babies, to have a whole front row sitting sideways on is a strange sight...

Can you tell me a bit more about the variety acts? Were there dancing girls at the Trocadero?

Yes, there were dancing girls, you name it. One week, I don't know if these names would mean anything to you but Tommy Trinder, Sophie Tucker and Larry Adler were the three acts on the bill, there were two feature films, one of which was *The Hurricane* with Jon Hall. Sid Field I can remember - I came in on my day off the week we had Sid Field in a revue called *Red Hot and Blue Moments*. He was utterly unknown. It was a touring revue and it was magic, and he did an act, Slasher Green, which variety fans will remember - one of the wonderful comic creations where he played what they called a spiv with a very long black

overcoat, a knotted white silk scarf and a turned-down black trilby. With his feed who was called Jerry Desmonde, he did this hilarious act and the place rocked. And it was full of chaps sitting there in long black overcoats, knotted white silk scarfs and trilbies. I'd never seen anything as funny and I watched every show, the whole week. I came down into the theatre for that and watched it and then I came in on my day off and watched it again.

It was the best, it was top variety, it was what they called a number one date. With this cine-variety, we had resident orchestras - Alfred Van Dam, big orchestras - who alternated between the Trocadero and the Elephant and Castle. The Elephant and Castle had a dance band run by a man called Teddy Joyce, a Canadian. He was incredibly handsome, enormously talented, very willowy figure, lean, black hair, who did what was called snake hip-type movements in dancing. We used to do Sunday concerts with him up from twelve o'clock till two where he got the same kind of adulation the Beatles got. My daughter, I would go and rescue her from Beatles concerts, weeping little girls coming out with their wet knickers and all that. That's exactly what I saw - in fact, we had to stop them because we couldn't seat people in the seats afterwards. With Teddy Joyce, he weaved a spell, his was much more deliberate. He knew what he was doing, he was a very smooth operator. There's no equivalent now to all the dance bands of the time, but they were a very big attraction and they all came and played the Troc, because it's in London, you see, so it's a number one, number one date in London. There weren't a lot of number one dates. There was the Palladium which was Mecca, and below that you had the Holborn Empire, the Finsbury Park Empire, the Troc, the State [Kilburn]. For a while there was Golders Green Hippodrome, nothing else being number one - number one being where they would pay money for the artistes.

And Saturday morning pictures?

For your sins, you had to take the kids. Dad was home on Saturday and Sunday and he didn't want the kids on his hands. He wanted to sleep. And we made a bit of money out of these kids even though it was only threepences and so on. And we had the serials and the cowboy films and the cartoons and so on. These Saturday morning things, they were monsters, they really were. At the Elephant, at the Troc, I announced something, I went up on the organ and was knocked off by a hail of oranges being thrown. We gave them oranges - "When are we going to get the bleeding chocolate?" sort of thing. It was Christmas.

In terms of comparison between live acts and celluloid, and the decline of music hall, was there a feeling that cinema wasn't the real thing? Did some people feel like that?

I don't think they felt like that. They lived alongside one another. Variety in those days was a family entertainment, although there weren't as many of them as there were of cinemas where people had the same seat every week and near as dammit saw the same show because those variety shows were so similar to each other, the great ones were few and far between, because there were such a lot of variety artistes.

 I think I was more affectionate towards variety than towards films because films came to you finished and polished by Hollywood. With variety every show was new, every performance was an adventure. You didn't know what was going to happen. An act could run over in time and you could have disputes. Noel Coward's *Red Peppers* is very spot on: the acts storming round to managers, "He ruined my act", "What does he know? He can't conduct a tramcar", and all this kind of thing. And you knew it was on the downward and you cherished the performers who were left who had no other skills, people who could balance a chair on their chin by one leg. What were they going to do?

 And then nudity. The nude shows started coming in with all the fancy titles and the families drifted away and it became the chyiking youths and the pensioners who really weren't very interested except that it was warm and they got the advantages of the seats. You saw that disappear and you knew it wasn't going to come back. Films changed, cinemas changed, but you knew it was going to stay in one form or another, but variety, you knew, was not going to come back. So it had this kind of runt of the litter feel about it. Emotionally, it had a greater hold on me anyway than films. I love films, I still do. I'd rather go to see a film than I would go to the theatre, but if there's a variety show anywhere I'd rather see that than anything.

Clifford Gentle

—————— *Clifford Gentle, born in 1926, became an actor, director and writer under the professional name of Clifford John Williams, and likes to see classic films at the National Film Theatre. He is also featured in Film Talk.*

How would you describe the Brixton Astoria?

You felt the Astoria was rather a smart place to go to because they served tea in the foyer. As you went in on the left hand side there was a cluster of tables with waitresses, afternoon tea. Ladies used to be sitting there. It was always rather grand because of the uniform of the doorman and I remember the manager would be almost bowing to the ladies and there was always an air of elegance at the Astoria.

You went in a big entrance hall. There was a box-office. There was a place which sold sweets - I remember especially the Turkish Delight bars were tuppence, the average was about tuppence, and usually I couldn't afford it because Mother would give me the exact money and I always walked. I never took the bus. Then there was a sweeping staircase as you went up. It was simply called the circle, not the dress circle. But I never sat there - that was rather grander up there and I think it was something like two shillings or half-a-crown to go up there, whereas the stalls, if it was the

Astoria Brixton: the inner foyer

afternoon it was ninepence, unless that was half price - I don't know. Then you went in and you looked up and there was that ceiling which was painted like a night sky with all these stars. In certain lights - I suppose it was the reflection around the auditorium - but they seemed to twinkle, very high up in a great dome of sky, with clouds and everything, and as your eyes looked down, you got great balconies that looked like Spanish houses. And on these balconies there was palm trees and windows and curtained alcoves and there was

The interior of the Astoria Brixton

a lot of gilding, I remember. It was all like an Aladdin's cave for a lad. And, of course, we had the man who used to come up on the organ...

What did the programmes consist of?

What happened is we always had a main feature and then we would have news, the trailers of the coming pictures which were often very exciting, and then there were the cartoons, and sometimes it was Easter or Christmas and we had a stage show, quite elaborately staged. I remember once there was a plantation one with "All the World Is Sad and Weary" and there were people on the plantation and quite an elaborate set with the trees and things like that. Then you went on to the second picture and then you left. You could, of course, sit round and see the other one again. There were some older people who used to sit there all day. It was warm, perhaps.

Was it quite common for kids to ask someone to take them in?

Always. You waited about and you hoped it was a lady with other children because you knew there would be no problem. Or usually a young man was all right. He'd say "Yes, mate." He got the tickets and in you'd go and you went wherever. But sometimes, with an older man, we learned to be a bit cleverer. We always thought there might be a bit of trouble if the man who took us in bought us a bar of chocolate or Turkish Delight. And at first one used to be delighted except that within a few minutes or half way through the first movie you'd have the arm on the thigh or arm round your shoulder or "Alright son". And then the hand would go up your shorts, and you got really bored with this kind of thing and you'd long for the end of the film because as soon as the lights went up they stopped.

What surprised me was, you would have thought that two of us would have prevented them but no. There was one man, a huge fellow, and he sat one of us either side of him and was on to both of us. How we worked this out was that after about half-an-hour or when this had started we used to say we had to go to the lavatory and find somewhere else to sit in the cinema. There was no more problem. And that was sad, I suppose, but it never worried us - you just found ways around it and thought this is how older men behave. But it wasn't.

You never thought of telling the manager or the usherette?

It never occurred to us. Strange, that. We'd been warned, mother had said, and when people said "What about a chocolate, son?", you would say "No, thank you", so you

Gone With the Wind *in the West End at the Empire Leicester Square in 1940*

didn't get involved with the chocolate. And you could get out of the business earlier - if you were quick enough, as you were going in one door into the auditorium, you could slip away and go in by another door. It all added excitement to going to the cinema.

The War didn't stop people going to the cinema by all accounts.

Sometimes they would leave if the siren went. They always told you when the siren went. Most people stayed. Initially people left but, as the thing went on, you thought, "I might be gone tomorrow. I might as well see the movie." It seemed more real than a war, the movies did. I remember we had this almighty blitz, because Goebbels had said if *The Great Dictator* opened in London we would have one of the biggest blitzes we'd ever had. And we did.

Was there a lot of audience feeling when they watched that?

A splendid film. Marvellous. There was applause all the time on lines - very strong feelings.

What about the news during the War?

It was about '33 when I started to go regularly and the news, the items were so often Hitler, those speeches, and that was more unreal than the films because you couldn't believe that anyone like that could be a threat because he was such a caricature. I remember a friend saying, "Oh, that maniac! Don't worry about that maniac." But it didn't occur to anyone that the whole nation would follow and do exactly what it was told. And Mussolini even more, when you saw pictures of him.

It was a little frightening at the time, and later when other places were occupied, but it only got real when we all had to go up to the Town Hall at Brixton and have our gas masks fitted. Then you began to wonder. And we had trial blackouts. I remember mother saying, "This is what it will be like if we have a war." I realise now why Mum didn't want me to go to *Things to Come*. So much of it did happen, because this is what happened.

People queued for the cinema in the dark?

Yes, you queued in the dark. And you had your torch and your gas mask. People were always leaving their gas mask in the cinema and you used to hear the usherettes calling "Madame!"

Did you see *Gone With the Wind* when it opened in the West End?

Of course. With all the hose pipes outside for the firemen in the Blitz. And there were lots of fire bombs. You had to step over the hoses to get in.

You went into the armed forces?

I did a year at RADA and then I volunteered. If you volunteered you could choose your service, so I volunteered under age because I didn't want to go into the Army. I wanted to go in the Navy.

Why?

Partly because it was a more glamorous uniform. But also the sea, and I hated the idea of being tied to a tank or anything like that, and travel. But it was also partly Lord Nelson and all that going on. The letter came. I was still at RADA and I said to Mother, "Oh, it's all right - I can go in the Navy." Mother's only comment was, "You would have to

choose the two professions which are all prick and no pence." She was right, too.

When you were in the Navy, did they give you film shows?

Indeed they did.

Where would they be?

Van Johnson and June Allyson in Two Girls and a Sailor *(1944)*

Down in the hole. In an aircraft carrier, where the aeroplanes are stored below, we didn't have that many aeroplanes so there was a large area which was just a great big space. And what they used to do, because there are two thousand men on an aircraft carrier, they put a huge big sheet up and half the ship's company sat on one side of it and half the other - so one of you saw it back to front. They showed it from one end, but they couldn't get everybody in front of it or, if they got everybody in front, it would have been too far away. Then we used to say, can we have it again and change ends? We did it sometimes.

What sort of films did you see?

Things like *Two Girls and a Sailor*. The Andrews Sisters were in a lot of things, Jimmy Durante and Gloria De Haven, June Allyson.

Do you think they deliberately chose cheerful ones?

Oh yes, oh yes.

They were to keep the spirits up?

Yes. And the one thing we got fed up with, they kept showing us the 1937 Coronation newsreel. Whether that was to keep us faithful to the King, but they gave it up eventually because there were only about three people out of two thousand sitting there. I asked for *Brief Encounter*, and got such a look. The petty officer said, "What! One of those women's pictures?" I was livid.

Did war films have a special meaning for people in the services?

I think we tended to want the girls and the musicals, to get away. I think we had enough of the forces. None of them seemed to convey the deadness and seeming pointlessness of so much of the forces' life. You fall in for these various parades, and they're so particular about uniform and you're in the middle of the Indian Ocean somewhere and they're worried about how your bow is tied and the RPO says, "Now then, you horrible little sailor, what are you?", and you're supposed to say "Horrible little sailor, sir!", otherwise you're in trouble.

Did you manage to see these various documentaries which were shown at home?

With very uplifting music played in the background, Vaughan Williams and sweeping hills and all that.

Did people take them seriously?

They got a lot of laughs, actually, because it was always an uplift tone - "...and here we have these brave girls working on the land..." There was one hysterical piece about the sailors and they were all saluting and this kind of thing. And it said, "The enemy may come but he won't get through you, Jack." It got a huge applause. Did it work? It may have worked.

At the end of the War, did you go back to RADA?

Yes. By that time most of my life was in the West End. I was always seeing movies over there with RADA friends. And then I married soon after that, married in '49.

And that was when you became interested in foreign films?

During the War, Studio One and Two at Oxford Circus, they always had the French movies and that's when we saw all the Gabin ones. They seemed so raunchy to us then - they were so specific compared with the English and American films of the time. The one about the circus, *Les Gens du Voyage* - that was spendidly done. And *Quai des Brumes*. And then later at the Academy was *Les Enfants du Paradis*. I remember there was a German *Woyzeck* which I saw just after the War at those cinemas in Tottenham Court Road, two besides each other.

The Continentale and the Berkeley?

Yes, and they always showed foreign films and I saw lots of German films there.

What were they like to go into?

They never seemed very clean. They were very dark, and it was girls who had problems there, not boys. My wife said they always got groped in there, so they devised this thing between them: if somebody started, they would light a cigarette and put it very near his hand and he usually got the message. Lois said you weren't safe anywhere because you'd get groped from behind - somebody would come from under the seats behind because some of the seats were broken away.

Leslie Hardcastle at the National Film Theatre

Leslie Hardcastle

Leslie Hardcastle, born in 1926, is Curator of the Museum of the Moving Image, following his many years in charge of the National Film Theatre, some of which he recalls in Working There.

I came from a theatre family. My mother and father were on the stage. They used to do musical comedy, variety, opera, because they were singers, and they had a straight act. The great big cinemas in those days used to have acts in the intervals.

Did you go with them at all?

On holidays. They saved up enough money to send me to a private school, a good Catholic school. When all my school chums were going to the south of France or Switzerland, I was going to Wallasey or some place up north. Sometimes they

The huge auditorium of the Davis Theatre Croydon

were on variety and I used to be with the Crazy Gang, Will Hay, Will Fyffe. But the person who got me into the whole thing of film was my grandmother, because she was an avid film-goer and she would go four times a week and take me with her. That was in the Croydon area. We had all the main cinemas: the ABCs, the Odeons, and the Davis Croydon, which was really one of the most beautiful cinemas, a fantastic cinema with a big restaurant and about 120 staff. I think it held about 2,500. My grandmother went to absolutely everything. She used to go to sleep. She'd go to sleep in the middle of the B picture and wake up in the middle of the news, which invariably had Adolf Hitler in it, go to sleep again and wake up in *Philadelphia Story* and then start saying it was a completely ridiculous film. She'd always get three films mixed up at the same time. She would complain about the dark and about the light and she talked in a loud voice: "Why can't we see where we're going?" and "This is a ridiculous film!"

So you didn't go with other kids when you were small?

I didn't really. I was always kind of a loner. I managed with a schoolboy friend to get in and see *King Kong*, because you weren't allowed to see *King Kong* and we did it as a dare.

How did you get in?

Through one of the exits. But people were sent to psychiatrists having seen *King Kong* because it was thought a terrible thing. When you see it now, it's a deeply moral film, quite innocent compared to the material of today. I remember queues, enormous queues, ex-soldiers - '14-'18 War - as commissionaires. And they were great characters and they used to stop little boys like me getting in the side entrance. And all the girls on the front desk selling the tickets thought they were Hedy Lamarr. I don't think British cinema was very good at that time.

I lived in London during the Blitz. I wanted to be a doctor and I was in the St. John's Ambulance Brigade. I used to see a lot of movies because I used to go as a St. John's Ambulance helper, and I was actually standing in the Davis Croydon the night the bomb came down, came through the roof and killed three people. Fortunately, it didn't go off, it just killed by impact - otherwise it would have been slaughter.

Did you get to see films while you were in the Navy?

I saw three films in the Navy about forty times each: one was about not catching venereal disease, one was about controlling flies, and the other was a film on "Careless Talk Costs Lives", terrifying because much of it actually came true - *Next of Kin*. My uncle, an actor, was in *Next of Kin*: he played the sergeant who talks too much and gets killed in the raid. *Next of Kin* actually came true at Dieppe where the enemy were working on advance information - the Germans were waiting for the Canadian forces when they arrived.

The most memorable film show I saw in the Navy was in

an aircraft carrier in the southern seas: we were going out to relieve the Pacific Fleet and I was one of 4,000 green sprogs on the Victorious. It was very hot and they used to at night open the airplane lifts to let the air go into the main hangar where all the men were bedded down. They used to hold film shows at the bottom of these lifts. I saw *Our Vines Have Tender Grapes* with Edward G. Robinson and Margaret O'Brien, the little orphan girl. (*Sentimental Journey* was another one about a little girl who lost her mother. They always used to show you sad films in the Navy - I don't know why.) The memorable thing about the film show was someone engaged the lift and it started to come down on the audience. Never was a cinema cleared so quickly.

"Careless talk costs lives": Stephen Murray in Next of Kin *(1942)*

Did the film industry help the services?

Yes. During the War there was the Royal Air Force Film Corporation, the Royal Navy and the Army Kinematograph Corporation. They had their own film units, run mainly by female projectionists. We used to see films all the time. And when we got to Japan after the Occupation, the American services had all the latest films before they were shown anywhere else. The Americans had good facilities for their service people. During the War, Hollywood played an enormous part in the propaganda side of the War and it helped fashion American opinion. I didn't mind the musicals and the escapist films, but when I saw Errol Flynn winning the Battle of Burma on his own, I got a bit fed up.

Did you get to see the British war films?

Yes. At the end of the War. Ealing was coming on stream.
There were dramatic documentaries like *Western Approaches*,
Fires Were Started, *The Bells Go Down*. I saw also *The Way
Ahead* and *Officers and Men*, directed by Carol Reed. The
civilian version you see was called *The Way Ahead*, but it's
based on *Officers and Men*, a much harder, tougher version
with the characters not exactly the same. It was not until
after the War that we saw German films like Leni
Riefenstahl's *Olympic Games* and *Triumph of the Will*. I realise
now we also saw quite a lot of Russian films during the War
but they were mainly about historic battles - *Alexander
Nevsky*, *Ivan the Terrible*, *Catherine the Great*. They were films
of great Russian heroes of the past, rather than World War II.

Where did you see those?

At the Tatler Cinema. Russian films were also shown in
London at the Scala Cinema. We used to go into the cinema
during the Blitz and V1 attacks and the sirens would sound -
I can't remember exactly what the manager said, something
like "Enemy action is imminent", and then he would say,
"The show's going on, but if you want to go to the air raid
shelter you can. The nearest one's around the corner" or
"We've got one under the stalls".

But the brave ones stayed. I remember seeing Lucille Ball
in an American musical during a major attack on Croydon
when they were dropping bombs all around us. It was at the
time when London had been equipped with anti-aircraft
rocket batteries. When those rockets used to go up, it used to
be quite terrifying. One night the rockets went up, we
thought successfully because they seemed to be shooting
down so many planes. We thought that the batteries had got
at least twenty-four planes. It was quite remarkable. The next
morning rumours went around that they weren't planes but
V1s or doodle bugs. The doodle bugs made a difference to
cinema going. People used to risk the bombs but the doodle
bugs did so much blast damage, audiences didn't risk it. They
went to the shelters.

A Russian film at the Tatler Charing Cross Road

Daisy Moore outside the new building on the site of the Ideal Cinema

Daisy Moore

Daisy Moore, born in 1928, still lives in Lambeth close to her birthplace, and keeps in touch with the church where she saw her earliest films.

Do you remember the first time you went to the cinema?

I don't remember the first time. I can remember going quite often because we lived near the Ideal. And we used to go Saturday afternoons - the tuppenny/threepence rush, we used to call it. My mother used to give us threepence and dare us to go in the tuppenny rush. If you went in the tuppenny rush, you had a penny to spend, and an old lady used to sit along the railings - I don't know if she had any legs even, she had this great big skirt - and she used to have peanuts and sweets and everything, so your penny used to go on that. Nine times out of ten you used to have to queue up round the side and, when they opened the door, you used to rush - that was the tuppenny rush and, if you got in, you were lucky.

What was the Ideal like?

It was a proper cinema. When my mum was well off and we could afford to go, we used to go on the Wednesday after we took stuff to the ragbag, got our money, and my mother would take us up when we came in from school. It would be threepence for my mum and a penny each for me and my brother.

The Ideal Lambeth

Did a minister run it?

It was definitely run by the church but I don't remember.

Who was keeping order?

It was Len Bradbrook. He was a black man. He was the only black man we knew as kids. Kids used to pull his hair because they thought it was wool and things like that. But he was the superintendent there to us kids.

Was he quite strict?

Oh yes, but he was a nice man. We never knew he was a coloured - he was just Len Bradbrook to us kids. He used to run the Boys Brigade, because from there they used to run the Boys' Brigade and the Girls' Life Brigade. I used to be in the Girls' Life Brigade, just for what you could get out of it. I used to go out for days with them. And I was with them when, a couple of days before the War broke out, we went to Brighton and they sent our parents telegrams saying if war was declared we would be sent home. We came home on the Wednesday and war was declared on the following Sunday.

Lots of activities used to go on there. On Friday night, it used to be silent films and it used to be a halfpenny and you used to get a mug of cocoa and a lump of bread and dripping. And we used to love that. I don't even think it was in the cinema. I've a feeling it was in the hall upstairs they used to take us. It was because we were all poor kids and it was a bit extra for us to get a bit of bread and dripping and a mug of cocoa.

Sometimes your mother used to take you to the cinema?

Yes, Mum used to go. I don't remember my dad going. The only time I remember my dad coming with us was when we used to go to the old South London Music Hall in London

Len Bradbrook and audience at the Ideal Lambeth

Road and we used to go to their gala night. And we used to queue up outside and he used to buy us an apple and orange each and some sweets, and we used to think we were ever so well off. And we used to go upstairs, and then you got a lucky draw number and they'd shine a light round and, if it caught you, you won a prize. It was good. I've a feeling that was on Wednesday or Thursday - it was in the middle of the week, I know. But Dad used to like the music hall and I follow him: I like all the sing-alongs and songs. It was good. I enjoyed my childhood. We never had a lot but what we did have was good parents.

You went out quite a lot?

My dad was a chauffeur when we were kids, so he had a car. He worked in it all the week, and weekends they used to let

Inside the Regal Kennington

my dad have it and take us out. So we used to go to the seaside at weekends. We weren't deprived of anything. Although we were poor, we never went without anything.

Do you remember any other cinemas before the War?

I remember the Trocadero. It was a big cinema but it was a bit further on. Living round here, you never ventured far from where you lived. We used to go to the Canterbury in Westminster Bridge Road.

Can you describe the Canterbury?

It was very highly decorated inside - ornate, as you would call it. I don't remember a lot about it but I know we used to go up there. When you're a kid, you don't notice - you just go up there, you're more interested in seeing the pictures.

What about Gatti's? Did you go there?

No. I can only remember going up there once. I remember they came round and sprayed you with a big spray to kill off all the insects and fleas. It was like what we use to kill the flies - it was a round thing with a plunger and a man used to come up and down the aisles...

Did you go to the cinema in the War?

I was eleven when the war broke out, so we never ventured far from where we lived for fear of raids and things like that. So, if you went anywhere, you only went local - the Regal in Kennington Road.

What was the Regal like?

It was big inside. When you're that age, you don't look - you're more interested in your bloke. We saw some good pictures up there. We never had a lot of money so we didn't

The Regal Kennington in 1937 (later the Granada)

go too often, because you didn't have the money to go. When we first got married, he was out of work - we used to go and get the dole money and get pies and mash and pease pudding and faggots and put them in a bag and sit in the pictures and eat them. I think everyone used to do the same.

Did you ever go to the West End?

No, it was a foreign territory, really, to you. Everyone was content to stay where you was. You all lived local.

Do you have any favourite films?

Years ago I liked *Millions Like Us* and *The Sullivans*. I can remember going to see *The Sullivans* up the Elephant and Castle. I was about sixteen and it was about five brothers. I was stupid at that age. I related to them. They got killed in the War. I can remember coming out there and crying my eyes out. I sat on a woman's window-ledge down Brook Drive and she came out and said, "What's wrong?" I didn't tell the woman I was crying over a picture because she would have thought I was crackers, but to me they were real.

And *Millions Like Us*. I'll always remember that, because of when they were laying a table out like we did because we were poor, a newspaper on the table. And my mum used to have little bottles for egg cups with the old stems and we'd put them on the table, and that happened in that film. I could relate to that.

Did you cry at the end of that?

No, it was a jolly film in a way. But *The Sullivans*, that sticks in my mind forever and a day.

Did you have favourite stars?

Yes. Greer Garson, *Mrs. Miniver*. And there was another

one where he loses his memory - it was about the First World War [*Random Harvest*]. I liked her in that.

What about comedy? Did you watch Charlie Chaplin?

I was never one for comedy. Charlie Chaplin grew up around here. In fact, I saw him just before he died. He fell over in Kennington Road, by the church by the Tube station. He'd come to London just to have a look around again - his family was in Switzerland - and he went to get up the pavement and he tripped and he bashed his face. His face was smothered in blood. I ran and picked him up. My daughter knew it was him. She said, "You're Charlie Chaplin", and he laughed and he just went like that. Soon after that, we read he'd been in London looking round his old haunts. Because he lived up where the Granada was - it used to be the Regal then. In Pownall Terrace he lived.

The Sullivans (1944): five sons serve on the same American battleship (Eddie Ryan, George Offerman, James Cardwell, John Alvin and John Campbell)

...and the mother learns that all have been killed in battle (Anne Baxter, Trudy Marshall, Selena Royle, Thomas Mitchell, Ward Bond)

Norman Cobden at the side of the former Majestic Clapham

Norman Cobden

Norman Cobden, born in 1932, lives in Borough and works for a computer company. His further memories appear in Film Talk.

Saturday morning club started us off going to the cinema. We used to go to the Clapham Majestic. We used to get the serials, you'd have the little cowboy film - Buck Jones and all this sort of thing. They used to have the competitions on the stage for all the children but the thing I remember they used to have most Saturdays was the biff bat: that was like a little

The Majestic Clapham as the Gaumont c1960 shortly before closure

table tennis bat with an elastic on and a little ball on the end, and everybody used to hit it out all the time to see who could hold it going the longest. Then they got to doing the tricks with it, but that was chaos in there. But everyone used to go and we used to go in and sing

We come along on Saturday morning,
    greeting everybody with a smile,
We come along on a Saturday morning,
    knowing it's all worthwhile,
As members of the GB Club,
We all intend to be
    good citizens when we grow up
And champions of the free,
We come along on Saturday morning.

We always sang that at the beginning, because they had like a compere come onto the stage before the films started. It was absolutely packed and you all sang it.

Do you remember starting to go to matinees?

I think when I really started was I got evacuated when the War started and I went to Slough and they had a little weeny cinema in the High Street and a big one up and I had another two aunts who moved out there, also from London, and they took me to the little cinemas. We had so many laughs in there, especially in the little cinemas. They were the ones if you were going to have a lark. You used to get audience participation. I can remember, we went to see a Western and I was enjoying it, I was quite small, but it was so bad that the audience started booing the hero and cheering the villain and it was hysterical. And from then on I just got the bug and went everywhere, literally.

In the War we used to go over to Regent Street, just past Oxford Circus, and you'd have the cartoon theatre there. We used to go out selling horse manure, just to get our money. We'd go in to see the cartoons, and you had all the coffee bars and everything. We used to treat ourselves to a waffle. To have a waffle was a big treat for us. That was when we'd earned a couple of bob.

What was it like going to the cinema during the War? Were there any special precautions?

Didn't worry at all. You got used to the bombing and everything. We used to go out as children, picking up all the shrapnel. As the bombs or the incendiary bombs fell we used to go out and pick up pieces of it. Some of it would still be hot. You wouldn't worry. It was just a way of life, really. You got used to it. And when you went to the cinema, if a warning was coming on, they'd show it on the screen: "There is an air raid warning just starting - would people wishing to leave, leave now."

Did you leave?

Nobody left. Just carried on. I think the attitude was: if you're going to cop it, you're going to cop it. It didn't matter where you was. You might as well be in there enjoying yourself as walking out trying to avoid it and still cop it.

There were some cinemas actually bombed.

But you were never safe anywhere. Like, they used to go down the Underground but they all got killed at Balham. And it wasn't always the bombs that done it. It was the blast that done a lot of it, whichever way the blast was going. The house behind us was bombed but the blast went all the other way. But we were in our glories as children. Bomb-damaged places, they were all our dens.

Was that the period that you were going almost every night to the cinema, during the War?

I think more when I left school I was going every night. When I was fourteen years old, because you had to leave school then. You just used to walk out of our doors, because you had no gardens, you just came straight out onto the pavement, and it would always be there, and we'd say we're going to the pictures and we'd go anywhere, literally, and it was every night then, twice on Sunday. Later on, we still went to the pictures a hell of a lot, but we'd go straight from the pictures to the Locarno Dance Hall in Streatham. But I love cinema, really.

You have to appreciate that when we got a little bit older we rarely paid to go to the cinema, which was the thing with most of us.

The Palladium Brixton circa 1946

How did you get in?

Bunked in. Easiest thing in the world. Clapham Majestic, you used to go down the side, an alleyway at the back, and you could open the back door as easy as anything with a bit of wire, only somebody would come out because it was a continuous performance then. You could walk in in the middle of a film and see it through again, not like today. So you sometimes would go round and somebody would come out. Once they came out, they couldn't shut the door because there was a crash bar, so the door would always be open. So you'd just walk in.

The Palladium Brixton, we used to have an usher there -

"Kipper" we used to call him because of his big feet. We used to see him riding a bike and his feet would be out. He was always ready for loads of us to bunk in. It was a massive passageway you had to get into. We used to send one in. Kipper used to come out after him and chase him. Now he'd chase him out the door and as he chased him out we'd all go in.

Kipper wasn't very bright.

No, Kipper wasn't very bright. Lot of other places were very, very tight. If they caught you, you never got prosecuted, you got thrown out. No one would ever turn round and give anyone a right hander like they would today. There was no verbal, really. What they said went. They were governors in there and if they said "Out you go", you got up and you went out. You never ever saw trouble in cinemas. People went to enjoy them. When we were younger people, we used to mess around a lot - when we used to go to the Brixton Astoria, which was lovely.

I was going to ask you about that.

Brixton Astoria, that was quite hard to bunk into. But you could get into it by going up the fire escape at the back, or you could get in sometimes down the side.

Was it always boys who did that?

Never the girls. Actually, about that time we never really bothered about girls. Even when I left school, at fourteen, at fifteen, we wasn't really interested in the girls. I know it sounds funny when you think about it now, but it wasn't really - we were all going about, we were having a good time. You had no money but you had a good time.

Did you ever spend money and queue up?

Yes, when I left school we used to stand outside the cinema and ask people to take us in. We could never get into an "A" film without asking someone to take us in or by going with an adult. But the people you always watched for was the people who were taking their girlfriend or their wife in. If you saw an elderly person coming in on their own, you would know straightaway they were going in the cheap seats. So you used to wait for the ones who looked like they were going to show an impression, so you'd ask them to take you in. You'd give them the ninepence or whatever it was to go in - you knew they were going in the dearer seats, so they used to pay the extra. You'd go upstairs with some of them, but they didn't want you near

Dr. Jekyll and Mr. Hyde at the Palladium in 1942

them because they were going to do their courting in the cinema sort of thing. You didn't care - you were in.

And it was very common to ask?

Yes, you never had any fears of it. You wouldn't dream of letting a child go out now and say to someone... it's a different sort of world. If there was an "X" on, naturally you couldn't get in. And there was an "H" then - horror film. *King Kong* was a horror film, but we bunked in to see that. We couldn't see it by getting anyone to take us in. Even your mother couldn't take you in, so you bunked in to see that. If they saw you, you were out - but then you'd try again the next night till you got to see it. Another one I can remember was Spencer Tracy, where he changed into the wolf sort of thing [*Dr. Jekyll and Mr. Hyde*, 1941]. We all bunked in to see that and it was deathly quiet. That was in the Palladium. We got by Kipper that night and had to go through the big curtains. One of my mates swung on it and it came down, and it was chaos. They all came after us and we all ran out. We had to bunk in the next night.

What do you remember of the Brixton Astoria? What are your impressions?

We always went downstairs and never upstairs, because to us it was posh upstairs and when you looked in there and you saw the people - especially in the afternoon, four-ish, they were all having their tea there. But if we wanted to see anything that we'd missed we'd go to the Brixton Pavilion or the Clapham Pavilion at which pictures changed three times a week.

Did you stick to the Brixton/Clapham/Camberwell area?

We'd say, "Let's go up to the Grand at Camberwell." You

used to get some real old ones there. They'd change about two or three times a week. The Golden Domes was up there. You'd go and see what was up there. "We've seen that. Let's go and see what's up there." We used to do the round.

I used to go to the Brixton Empress when I was younger, always up in the gods. We used to go and see Tod Slaughter in there - *The Old Dark House* - and you used to have a bit of

The Golden Domes Camberwell in the Fifties as the Essoldo

a shout, and [the manager] Mr. Smith - he used to see we were quiet in there. He would come over and that was it. I saw a good Australian film there. That was *Forty Thousand Horsemen*. I thought it was a brilliant film - all about the Australians in the First World War.

Did you keep within walking distance?

Usually, although we walked quite a way, we walked a long way. But you had enough cinemas in our area to cater for anyone. Brixton we had the Astoria, the Palladium, the Brixton Pavilion. We also got a film on Sunday at the Empress. On Brixton Hill we had the New Royalty which later became the Clifton. Then we had the Clapham Majestic and the Clapham Pavilion. You had one at Stockwell and at Camberwell you had the Golden Domes and the Grand. You didn't need to venture really. Streatham would have it and we'd have it.

You hear about fleapits. Now the New Royalty, that was a fleapit. And we used to be in there watching the film and a

woman used to come spraying above your head with the DDT.

Was that a very strong smell?

Creased you. But they did it all over you, they didn't care - they just used to come round and spray. No one took no notice - you were seeing your film, you were in fantasy land.

When did you start going with the girls to the cinema?

About seventeen, I suppose, about '49 or '50. We used to go mostly on Sunday afternoons with the girls. Night-time we never used to go out a lot with them. So cliquey, my friends were.

So your group of friends would go with a group of girls?

Yes, we'd always be together, very rarely on our own. The same when we were in the dance hall. I went in the army in 1951, then I came out, but we used to go to the cinema then. Still no money so we'd bunk into the pictures. I was going more to Streatham then. We'd go to the dance hall, the Locarno. No one's got enough, so we'd pay threepence for a balcony ticket and we'd look over and see if any of our mates were downstairs. We'd say, "Bring us up a ticket" - again, we were bunking in because they used to have a woman at the top of the stairs and she'd clip the ticket or look at the ticket. They'd bring us up spare tickets so we'd walk down and spend the rest of the night in the dance hall.

Was that your main form of entertainment?

There was nothing really else to do. We never had television, so if you wanted to see anything you went out to the cinema.

Suzanne Waite outside the Coronet Elephant and Castle, the former Elephant and Castle Theatre

Suzanne Waite

Suzanne Waite, born in Walworth in 1937, recalls her early years around the Elephant and Castle. Her memories also appear in Film Talk.

My mum and dad liked the pictures. They used to go twice

The Elephant and Castle Theatre in 1960

a week, always up the Elephant. I was born in Marsden Road but before I was a year old they moved to Guinness Trust on Kennington Park Road. It was rather posh then because they had their own bathroom and inside toilet. Nobody had a bathroom and inside toilet. And right bang opposite the Guinness Trust was the Princes Theatre, so we were running across there all the time to the pictures. So really at that time I think it must have been three times a week to the pictures: the Princes, always up the Elephant, the Elephant and Castle [Theatre], and always up the Troc.

Did you go to special children's shows?

Oh, yes. I never missed one. Up the Troc. I don't think the Elephant did a Saturday morning. Saturday morning shows, they were smashing: the kids used to holler and scream and shout and throw things. You used to get cartoons and a main film. They'd start about half-past nine and finish about half-twelve. Oh, that was my highlight, Saturday morning pictures. Sixpence, I think.

Some Saturday mornings they would have stars there - I can remember Anne Crawford, Pat Roc.

Was there a period when cinema-going was a regular habit?

Yes, I used to go twice a week. Two nights a week cinema and Tuesdays and Fridays would be Brixton Empress and Camberwell Palace - that was live stage shows. My dad took me to all those.

The Elephant pictures, you queued like mad in those days and it was under the arches you queued and there would be rows and rows of alligator queues. That was for an evening performance. It took forever to queue up to get into the Elephant and Castle. But the Trocadero opposite was a much bigger cinema and so really you only queued along the road, perhaps halfway up going towards New Kent Road - that was the queue, I think, if you wanted upstairs. Then, if you wanted to go downstairs, you queued round a big pub on the corner called the Rockingham pub that went round into Newington Causeway.

One of the main things was seeing all the buskers outside. When we went to the Elephant and Castle there was always one there. They used to call him "Mutton Eye". He used to have a load of rusty keys and his song was "Lock my heart and throw away the key". He'd throw these keys and everybody used to grab them. And they used to love him. He was scruffy. We were told - it was probably a rumour - that he was found dead and he was worth thousands.

Saturday morning at the Troc Elephant and Castle

What time did you go?

I think we always left home about half-past six. It never used to be a long night. It was all over by half-past nine to a quarter to ten.

Do you remember the cinema manager?

Yes. They were always there. You could see them, not like today when you have to hunt for the manager of anything. The manager was always there on the front and the commissionaires, the usherettes with their little torches and the girls used to stand down the front with their trays of choc ices and the rest of it. Page boys, always young boys with their hats, always small. The toilets - I can still remember the smell of them, a little string to pull.

Do you recall turns on stage at the Troc?

There were always turns on there - not every week. The Troc had a really good stage - a great, great stage. I can remember they used to bring down a great big sheet and whoever the turn was might sign and you'd sing with this sheet.

The Troc was a very big cinema. A beautiful organ used to come up during the interval.

Did it bother you to go in half-way through?

Strangely enough, no. I think everybody used to go in halfway unless you queued like mad - then they used to try and organise it so that everybody went in at the beginning. But it never really worried us to go in half way and you could sit round again and see the next half.

Where did you sit?

My dad halfway back, downstairs. He didn't like going upstairs. We always sat halfway back, always in the middle and downstairs - I think because at the back was all the courting couples, down the front was all the kids.

Were they quiet in the cinema?

If you went in the afternoon matinee, then it used to be very, very noisy - you would hear all the time "Sssh...sssh!" When I went at the evening time, with my parents, then it was much quieter then.

How did you know what was on?

They showed you the coming attractions of the next week. Then we'd say, "Yes, we'll see that." The South London Press would tell you what was on local. And I used to buy Picture Show. That would tell you what was coming on. They used to sell the Picture Show in the auditorium. We used to buy that for each week. Picturegoer, Picture Show, Film Fun - we used to have them all.

Was there a special atmosphere in cinemas during the War?

During the war-time when all the local people - sons, husbands, boyfriends - were in the War abroad, they would bring up their picture on the cinema screen, give their name. The organ would come up and play and up would come this wonderful picture of an airman, sailor, soldier, whoever, and his name would come up and then they would put the name of whoever requested this. And then the fellow on the organ would play the tune and everybody would sing. It was lovely.

Sometimes the lights would go up and they would mention different people's names and there might be a soldier or an airman sitting there and they'd be welcomed back home. Yes, it was a family atmosphere - especially being local, we all knew each other.

One I did go an awful lot to with an aunt - she lived at Brixton and her flat backed onto the Astoria. That was one of my favourites. We would have tea on the terrace looking out over Brixton - a real waitress with a little black dress and a white lace apron with a cap. I would have ice cream in silver bowls, you used to have that with wafers, and my aunt always had a pot of tea and cakes. And then we would go and see the film.

What happened during air raids?

Sometimes they would send somebody out if the bombs were very near, then they would send everybody out. My mum and dad would go straight into the Rockingham pub and when it was all clear they would all go back into the pictures.

I can remember the Princes Theatre being bombed out completely. We came out of the shelters one morning and there was the Princes no more. It was gone. That was sad. I can still see the smoking embers. That was a very nice cinema, very wide in the front - all steps so you had plenty of room to walk into the auditorium.

Were there any special safety precautions?

Yes. They used to drop a safety curtain - a great, big, thick, white fire curtain. They had to drop that. Often we were turned out of the cinema but you could go back in.

Did more people go to the cinema?

No. I can remember sometimes they were quite empty. A lot of people were maybe frightened to go out when the Blitz was really bad. I can remember spending months more down the shelter than anywhere. There was a time when you wouldn't even dare come out. You were down there day and night, and it was awful. I think that they shut the cinemas down for a time when it was really bad.

Did people make comments during the news?

Not so much comments as they would clap as different items came up - I can see Churchill, Eisenhower...

The news was very important and I remember we children weren't allowed to be in there for the news one time: that was the Belsen camps. But I peeked in and it was awful. But I used to enjoy the Pathe News very much, ordinary times.

Did you get into "A" pictures?

Perhaps when I was around twelve or thirteen if I borrowed Mum's high heels, then I might get into "A" films. They were very strict about that. I think the only way most kids got in was by bunking in when somebody opened the back doors.

Did you bunk in?

Yes. And got thrown out. When you're with your friends, the gang - if they did it, you did it. But I think the kids that did that, they never got taken to the pictures. I never really had to do that because my mum and dad were always there to take me to the pictures. I can remember as people used to come out these great big exit doors at the back, if somebody came out and left it a little bit ajar, somebody would put their feet in and that was the way you got in. I can remember this once getting in this back door at the Elephant and Castle but it actually brought you to the front of the stage and all the lights were on and [somebody yelled] "Out! Don't come back!"

Did you do your courting at the cinema?

We used to go to the Regal in Kennington Road - it's called the Granada now, bingo. If it was a nice evening we would go over to Hyde Park, walking around, but we didn't have such nice weather in those days. The winter was much longer than the summer. Yes, mostly pictures in the back row.

Was going to the cinema a special occasion?

It wasn't a special thing for me. It was an everyday thing. I'll tell you one special thing - my mother's mother treated us all one day. It's one of my earliest recollections of going to the West End cinema. She took me and some of my cousins. It was the film *The Bells of St. Mary's* with Bing Crosby and the only way of getting into that was about ten o'clock in the

A West End treat: The Bells of St. Mary's *(1945) with Bing Crosby and Ingrid Bergman*

morning. And I remember really enjoying that. We came out in the afternoon. It was brilliant sunshine. But that was wonderful, *The Bells of St. Mary's.*

Were you aware of the cinemas changing in your area?

I think the first sign was when there was nobody queueing any more. They all had televisions. And then they started going off to bingo halls. When they first put the Granada to a bingo hall, my dad had died then but I can remember thinking he would turn in his grave if he knew what had happened to his cinemas. But bingo never caught on at the Troc or the Elephant.

What was the last time you went to the Troc?

It was when I did have children - I lived in the Old Kent

Road and sometimes I would pick them up from school at four o'clock and I would take them to the pictures. But that didn't last very long because television was in then. People couldn't afford the pictures so much. You were happy with television. We had it on Radio Rentals, you had to pay every week - you couldn't do that and the pictures. Pictures with the children was a rare occasion.

The last time we did go as a family to a cinema in the West End, my son Lewis was eight and my family was having a get-together and it had to be fancy dress so I said, "Oh, we'll dress Lewis as Oliver." We couldn't find a picture of Oliver so I said, "We'll all go over and see the film." It cost a bomb to go in and see *Oliver!* Then the lights have gone up and Lewis says, "I want an ice-cream." So I said to my husband Charlie, "Get the two kids one and we won't." He was shocked at the price of ice creams in there. Then Lewis wanted something else. I said, "You're having nothing else, so shut up." Lewis said, "I hope you forget what he looks like" - he knew we were only going to see what Oliver Twist looked like. "Oh, you naughty boy!" That was the last time we all went to the cinema. It cost a bomb.

What was special about cinema-going?

When I was a kid, it was just a good night out. Everybody used to flock out of the cinema and all fight to get on the tram car and it was all part of the fun - I enjoyed it. I can only say I miss it from those days. I don't miss it from now.

Mo Heard in the Hollywood Studio area of the Museum of the Moving Image

Mo Heard

Mo Heard, born in 1940, went into acting as a career and is now in charge of the Actors' Company at the Museum of the Moving Image. She is also interviewed in Working There and Film Talk.

We lived in Catford, the edge of Catford, in Lewisham in South-East London. My mum went to Taunton to have me because it was during the Blitz in 1940. I'm the only child. I have no brothers or sisters and my dad was away in the army. My mother went to the pictures twice a week and I'm sure she took me. My earliest memories are going to all the cinemas in that area: there were three in Catford and there were three in Lewisham and I went to all of them. My mother took me to "A" films - Joan Crawford and Bette Davis and all those. I think my earliest memories are round about 1945, 1946. I remember seeing *It Always Rains on Sundays* and all those British films. We used to go after nursery school. What I do remember is my mother used to buy the ice-cream in the Co-Op, so it must have been at a period when you couldn't get ice-creams in the cinemas or they were cheaper outside, and we used to take those with us.

About ice-creams in cinemas, we used to get tubs and they were very, very hard and you used to peel round the top of the cardboard tubs until it was halfway down and the ice-cream inside was so hard you could hold the tub and lick it like an ice-cream cone. And I always remember the tops - you never had wooden spoons in those days, you took the top off and folded it in half and used that as a spoon.

I remember coming out and it was dark and we used to walk

home and always stop at the fish and chip shop and buy threepenneth of chips. I was completely hooked by all those films.

Did any films ever frighten you as a child?

I remember very vividly certain frightening scenes but I do not remember what films they were from. They must have been "A" films but obviously, because I was so young, I would not know what the title was. I remember there was a woman in a bedroom and she heard the glass breaking downstairs and she went down the staircase and her silhouette was against the wall and she had a flowing nightgown on. I don't know who it was. And she came down the stairs and I think whoever it was at the bottom reached up and murdered her or something. And there was another film where some woman was walking down a crunchy gravel path in a park or a garden at night and there were footsteps following her in this crunchy gravel. And then she stopped and they stopped.

The Prince of Wales Lewisham circa 1946

In those days it was continuous performance, so you'd go in and move along the row and then you'd plonk down and you might be in the middle of a B picture. How at the age of four or five could you pick up a story like that? And then you'd go through the newsreels and the ads and the rest of it and then you'd get the A picture and then you'd come to the B picture. And the moment it got to the point where we came in, my mother would nudge me and say "This is where we came in." And up you'd get and walk out. We didn't have to leave but I suppose she didn't want to sit there any longer.

Did you go to children's shows on Saturday mornings?

I went to Saturday morning pictures at the Prince of Wales [Lewisham] and the Plaza [Catford]. I became an ABC Minor - "We're Minors of the ABC and every Saturday we go there

... and shout aloud with glee", etc., etc. I remember when the manager - or whoever used to get up before the films on stage and get us to sing bouncing ball songs - asked if there were any children who wanted to get up and do tap dances and things, I got up with a friend and we sang "I'm Forever Blowing Bubbles". I think I must have been only about seven. It must have been painful.

And, of course, the terrible noise that all the yobby kids made! And my friend and I used to sit near the back and we were terribly classy because we knew about cinema and we watched the films. Every time in the films they came to the dialogue, suddenly mayhem, pandemonium broke out, and we would sit there and we'd go "Shut up! Be quiet!" and tell off these kids around us. Once we obviously chose the wrong people to tell off, because they chased us afterwards down the High Street and were going to beat us up.

When I was older I would say I was brought up on the American musical and I just dreamt and fantasised about being Vera-Ellen and Cyd Charisse, Debbie Reynolds, Mitzi Gaynor - all those actresses with their very tight waists and their big belts and their dresses and skirts that went out and there were all those petticoats. When someone like Mitzi Gaynor did a twirl and the skirts sort of rose up, they had about six miles of thick petticoats on underneath.

Did you ever try and copy hairstyles and make-up?

I don't think so. I used to draw ladies with dresses like that on my school books and all over the place. I do remember in Catford there was a shoe shop on the corner of Wildfell Road and Rushey Green and it was called Vyners of Hollywood. And in the windows, literally stacked from floor to ceiling, were thousands of shoes, and they were all glamour shoes. And they had sort of twelve-inch wedge heels and they were made of snake skin. And they had peep toes and high ankle

The Queens Rushey Green, later renamed Gaumont, circa 1946

things. And I used to drool over that shop. I never ever met anyone in the street who ever wore anything like that. And I really wanted shoes like that. By the time I got to the age of being able to wear shoes like that, they'd disappeared.

I used to go to matinees in the holidays with friends. And I remember my friend and I, we must have been about ten, queueing up for hours to see this wonderful film at the Queens in Rushey Green. It was next to the Lewisham Hippodrome. It was the most beautiful cinema. It was very tiny. There were a few marble steps up to these gold-handled glass doors and then there was a central paybox. I think you went in either side. I remember low ceilings, very narrow inside, and lots of brass. There was a brass rail halfway down with a red plush curtain and presumably the expensive seats were behind and the cheaper ones in front. On the left-hand side, there were only three or four seats against the wall before the aisle, just a few seats down the side. I can see it now: it was quite narrow but tall and arched, so it was definitely a mini electric palace.

And I remember queueing for hours to see this film with

my friend and when we finally got in and were sitting there watching this film, the usherette came up with a torch and shone it on me. And there was my dad who was terribly cross because he'd obviously got very worried that I hadn't come home. He knew that I'd gone to the pictures and he'd come to find me and fetch me out.

Talk about being shown up in the cinema, I remember going to the Gaumont at Lewisham with my mum and my aunt and it was in the afternoon and just a few people in there, and they'd bought the cheaper seats at the front. And I remember my aunt, who was always a bit of a girl, she said, "Come on, there are loads of seats - let's move back." And we moved back and, of course, the usherette came and told us off and made us move forward again. There was no one sitting at the front at all and I was very embarrassed by that.

The Gaumont Lewisham: 1932 view of main foyer

What was the Gaumont like as a building?

The Gaumont at Lewisham was a palace. We never, ever went in the circle at the Gaumont. It was obviously far too expensive for my mum. We always went in the stalls. And what I do remember is queueing to get into a film that everybody wanted to go and see. And once you'd bought your ticket, on each side of the foyer they had these "corrals" and you would go into this corral which had a brass rail and you would queue inside that. And then they would let you into the back of the stalls where they had more corrals, which I've never seen anywhere else. The cinema was enormous - I think it must have had about six aisles. Right at the back, you had the low wall of the back

1935 exterior

seats and then you had this step up away from the back aisle and that had brass rails around it. So you were let into one of these corrals where you stood and you were higher than the seats so you could watch the film. And then they would gradually get you out and seat you.

And one other thing: some B picture star, Faith Domergue, had appeared at the Gaumont and there she was coming down the stairs and my mother said, "Go on, go and ask her

1932 view of auditorium

for an autograph." And she got my diary out and I went up and this film star used my back to write her autograph, and there was a flash, a photographer, and my mother discovered it was the local paper. And she said, "You're going to be in the local paper." But I never was.

Allen Eyles

Allen Eyles, born in 1941, was brought up in Tooting Bec and Streatham. He became a teacher and then a film historian, developing a specialist interest in cinema buildings. He also contributes to Film Talk.

My parents weren't keen filmgoers but they would take me occasionally as a treat and I remember some of the films that I saw - particularly ones that were in colour like *King Solomon's Mines*, *The Elusive Pimpernel*, *Captain Horatio Hornblower R.N.*, *Where No Vultures Fly*... And I remember seeing *Cargo to Cape Town*, which was a black-and-white war film.

A cause of nightmares: Eric Portman as the killer descended from a notorious public hangman in Wanted for Murder *(1946)*

One of the films I saw early on gave me nightmares, which was the only time this ever happened to me. I don't think my parents would have taken me to see this film particularly - I think it must have been on as a supporting feature to something they thought I would like. But it was a British film in black-and-white that had to do with a man who went around strangling women in parks at night and it had something to do with the public hangman with some kind of

Allen Eyles in the foyer of the former Regal Streatham, now Cannon

climax on a lake in the dark, and this had quite a nightmarish effect on me.

Other than that, films didn't make any great impression on me until one Easter holiday in 1952 when I was at a loose end and my mother said, "Here, take some money and go off to the pictures." At that time we were living in Tooting Bec and for some reason I went to a small cinema at Tooting Broadway called the Vogue, possibly because it was opposite one of the entrances to Tooting market, where I used to go in and buy old comics from one of the stalls, and I was attracted

Auditorium of the Vogue Tooting

by the stills outside. That particular day they had an early Marx Brothers film called *Monkey Business* on, with one of those Technicolored Universal Westerns which was *Wyoming Mail* or *Comanche Territory* or some such title. And I went in and saw this programme and I thoroughly enjoyed it.

Films that made an addict: Monkey Business *(with Harpo, Zeppo, Chico and Groucho Marx)*

I was also struck by the trailer for the film showing later in the week which was *Three Godfathers*, a Technicolor western with John Wayne, which made great note of the fact that it was directed by John Ford, "a great director of westerns". It

looked very exciting from the trailer so I went back and saw that and loved it. It was showing with Chaplin in *Tillie's Punctured Romance*. And it was seeing those two programmes in that one week that really developed a passion in me for going to films. Because thereafter I went as often as I possibly could.

Did you ask adults to take you into "A" films?

Yes, the "A" certificate was a barrier to going to films I wanted to see. I remember when I first became interested in films there was a "U" certificate James Mason spy film called *Five Fingers* which seemed to be showing everywhere with an "A" certificate supporting film except at the Clifton Brixton Hill. I made an effort to go over from Tooting Bec to Brixton

Films that made an addict: Three Godfathers *(Pedro Armendariz, Harry Carey Jr. and John Wayne)*

Hill because it was a double "U" programmme there and I could get into it.

The supporting features were often most inappropriate to the main films. My father took me to *High Noon* with Gary Cooper and it was showing with a revival of *Edward My Son*, a film with Spencer Tracy which was extraordinarily tedious for a boy of my age. And I didn't understand why you never saw Edward, the son in the title. Everybody talked about him but he never appeared. To a boy of eleven, this was purely baffling and I had really come to see Gary Cooper shoot it out and I didn't want all this talking.

When I couldn't get my parents to take me to the "A" films that I wanted to see, I started getting people to take me in. I would usually look for a woman, I think. I never had any trouble going in with people. But I felt obliged to sit with them. I felt if I sat somewhere else on my own the usherettes would know I shouldn't be there and I might get thrown out.

I remember on one occasion after we moved to Streatham I got into a film called *Second Chance* with Robert Mitchum and the woman I was with had very bad eyesight and we sat on the front row. It was like looking up the side of a cliff, this terrible view of the screen, and after a while I had to excuse myself and sit somewhere else, because I just couldn't stand it.

I think my greatest coup in that area was when I noticed *King Kong* was being revived at the Classic South Croydon and this I'd never seen. It was "X "certificated but over the border in Surrey it had been given an "A" certificate. I decided to take a chance on it and I hopped on a 109 bus which stopped outside the Classic and got off and hoped to get somebody to take me in because it was quite an investment in bus fare going that far. But I got in straight away and felt pleased to have seen an "X" film so young. And, of course, it was a very impressive first "X" film to see.

Also I found at the Brixton Pavilion they would often let me in to "A" films on my own just to boost the numbers inside. So I used to make a habit of going down there although it wasn't a very nice cinema inside. But one day I went down to see a film called *Larceny Inc.* with Broderick Crawford and the cashier said, "I'm sorry I can't let you in today. We've heard the inspector's coming round." So this film was always on my list as one I wanted to catch up with. And when it turned up on Channel Four recently I recorded it, but I haven't wanted to watch it in case it's disappointingly bad and I shouldn't have worried about it all these years.

Did you enjoy the whole experience of being in the cinema?

Not in terms of lots of people being there. It was actually an irritation when the cinemas were full, because when you were small if you had to sit behind adults you had to perch on the end of the seat and twist your neck to see around them. And that was when there was invariably cigarette smoke drifting into your face.

And when there were queues, as there were for some of the *Doctor* films at the Streatham Astoria, once you actually gained access to the stalls you were kept waiting on a raised side section, a side passage. So you were just gazing at this sea of heads hoping that someone would get up and go and vacate a seat. And then the usherette would place you. If you went as a family you couldn't all sit together. Or you could wait until enough seats became available. Queues often meant getting seated in the middle of the film because these were the days of continuous performances. I used to hate that because I never liked seeing a film from the middle. And I remember my father would touch me on the shoulder and say, "Time to go - we saw this bit before." And I'd say, "Can we stay a little bit longer?" I wanted a ten minute overlap, or preferably stay to see the rest of the film again to have seen it properly.

How did you know what was on in particular cinemas?

A lot of shops had posters outside for what cinemas were showing. I noticed these and would respond to them. Once I was cycling round near Wimbledon and I saw a lot of posters in a rather lurid yellow for a cinema called the King's that was showing Fritz Lang's *Hangmen Also Die*. It was very luridly described and had pictures of nooses and things. This rather tempted me. I cycled back home and then went out to Wimbledon. I assumed because this film had been so widely publicised there would be enormous crowds there. When I got there there was hardly anybody else in the place at all. It was a very dusty, murky sort of cinema - I think it was bare floorboards. It wasn't the kind of cinema I ever wanted to go to again.

My parents had the local newspaper so I used to study that when it came out every week. When we moved to Streatham when I was twelve or thirteen, I'd look at What's On in London in the library and see what was showing more widely. I was interested in the programmes of the Classics at places like Chelsea and Baker Street and Notting Hill Gate.

What sort of programmes did they do?

Well, it was old films but they showed them properly and

they were well run cinemas like the Classic at Tooting Bec. And after I'd seen that first Marx Brothers film and first John Wayne film I really started going to all the films they were in. One way of catching up with the Marx Brothers was to keep an eye on what was showing at the Classics. The furthest I ever went, and it was quite a trek, was to see the Marx Brothers in *Go West* at a Classic cinema called the Vogue at Stoke Newington.

What year did you move to Streatham?

In 1953 or '54. The local cinemas there were the Astoria and the Regal. And there was this closed cinema at Streatham Hill which had been the Gaumont which I passed by and often wondered about and which eventually re-opened while I was living in Streatham. From where I lived it was quite logical to go into Brixton or Croydon because they were on the main bus routes out of Streatham.

Also, because my father worked for the railways I could travel very cheaply by train and I used to favour the Cameo at Victoria. I think I went to Victoria first for the Biograph because I noticed from the local press advertising that it was showing some obscure John Wayne films, early B Westerns he'd made, with titles like *Randy Rides Again* and *The Man from Utah* that I wanted to see, and they never played anywhere else. So I went up there and they were very poor films but I enjoyed seeing them and it became another cinema that I went to. But the seats in there were very tight against each other and there wasn't any proper arm rest between them and I noticed a great deal of movement of the audience there, in the late Fifties, early

Sixties. It had a very flat rake and although it had a large screen it was difficult to see the bottom of it. And you'd find whole rows of patrons continually standing up to let someone in or out and constant activity. Men would come and sit next to you for about five minutes and when there was no favourable response they would get up and try somewhere else. I remember I was very keen to see a film called *Paris Blues* again and I got so fed up trying to watch it under these conditions that I went and stood at the back and watched it well over the heads of the audience.

But the Cameo also showed films which didn't seem to play anywhere else. I saw lots of old Warner Bros. films there - they seemed to show two or three a month. I saw James Cagney films like *The Oklahoma Kid*, *Each Dawn I Die* and *Torrid Zone* and some of the Bogarts. The Cameo had very short programmes. They showed the film and then maybe a cartoon and the newsreel and the ads in rapid succession, and then the film came straight on again - there was hardly any pause. It was a very efficiently run cinema. I always enjoyed going there. It had a clock up in the entrance saying if you come in now you'll leave at a certain time. When the film came on again you would always see somebody a bit startled as though there should be a

Programmes for JANUARY

Day	Stars / Film	Times	Day	Stars / Film	Times
Thurs. Dec. 31 For 3 days	Robert Mitchum Teresa Wright **PURSUED** (A)	11.15 1.10, 3.5 5.0, 7.5 9.10	**Sunday Jan. 17** For 4 days	Monty Woolley : Thelma Ritter Marilyn Monroe **AS YOUNG AS YOU FEEL** (U)	11.0 12.25, 1.55 3.25, 4.55 6.25, 8.0 9.35
Sunday Jan. 3 For 4 days	James Cagney : George Raft Jane Bryan **EACH DAWN I DIE** (A)	11.0 12.40, 2.20 4.5, 5.45 7.35, 9.20	**Thurs. Jan. 21** For 3 days	Cary Grant : Priscilla Lane Raymond Massey **ARSENIC AND OLD LACE** (A)	11.5 1.5, 3.0 4.55, 6.55 9.0
Thurs. Jan. 7 For 3 days	Humphrey Bogart Ida Lupino **HIGH SIERRA** (A)	10.45 12.25, 2.10 3.55, 5.40 7.30, 9.20	**Sunday Jan. 24** For 4 days	Joel McCrea : Evelyn Keyes Marius Goring : Roland Culver **ROUGH SHOOT** (U)	11.0 12.40, 2.20 4.5, 5.45 7.35, 9.20
Sunday Jan. 10 For 4 days	Victor Mature : Coleen Gray Glenn Langan **FURY AT FURNACE CREEK** (U)	11.0 12.40, 2.20 4.5, 5.45 7.35, 9.20	**Thurs. Jan. 28** For 3 days	Richard Widmark Dana Andrews **THE FROGMEN** (U)	10.45 12.25, 3.55, 5.40 7.30, 9.20
Thurs. Jan. 14 For 3 days	Joseph Cotten : Valli Orson Welles : Trevor Howard **THE THIRD MAN** (A)	11.0 12.55, 2.55 4.55, 7.0 9.5	**Sunday Jan. 31** For 4 days	Humphrey Bogart James Cagney **OKLAHOMA KID** (U)	11.0 12.25, 1.55 3.25, 4.55 6.25, 7.55 9.30

Programmes and times are subject to alteration. See Entertainments Column in the "Evening News," "Star" and 'Standard.'

CAMEO
Telephone : VIC 6588
VICTORIA
OPPOSITE UNDERGROUND
Famous For Famous Films
JANUARY --- 1954
★ "LET'S GO TO THE PICTURES" ★

supporting feature, and they'd get up and go just as the credits started. Sometimes if I liked a film I would sit through it twice because it didn't take up that much time.

What about 3-D films?

Of course, while I was going to the cinema in the early Fifties this was the great era of technological change. The first 3-D film that I noticed came to the Eros in Croydon, a film called *Sangaree*, so I went off with a friend to see it. There was a notice that came up on the screen saying that these glasses - which were proper grey polaroid glasses, not the cheap cardboard things - had cost some huge amount to make each, so would patrons be sure to return them when we left the theatre? So my friend and I tried to get away with these valuable items through the furthest exit. The usherettes were waiting for us and leapt out and snatched them back from us.

Was 3-D a great experience?

It was always advertised as a lion in your lap, spears thudding past your head, and this kind of thing. And I realised it was like looking through a glass window: everything beyond that glass window was stunningly in depth but nothing actually came any further than the screen. So it wasn't as involving as they made out, but I loved it.

I remember when CinemaScope turned up, the nearest place it played was at the Granada Thornton Heath, and I went to see *The Robe*. When I went in there they were showing the trailer for *King of the Khyber Rifles*. It's hard to convey this now but when you were used to this rather tall, small screen, to come in to a place and see this panoramic screen was really startling. And also the stereophonic sound, with the speakers around the auditorium, was very impressive. There was a short called *Vesuvius Express* which had a train rushing across the screen and it seemed to rush down one side of the auditorium as far as the sound went, across the screen and up the other side.

There was always a rush to get out of the Granada Thornton Heath at the end of a performance, as soon as it was clear the film was ending. This was to avoid being at the end of the huge bus queues that used to line up right outside the cinema. The place was deserted even before the National Anthem started.

A personally inscribed portrait from The Ladykillers *following the Peter Sellers' guest appearance at the Astoria Streatham*

Did you see any personal appearances by the stars?

Occasionally you would have celebrity appearances at the Streatham cinemas. The first one I noticed, they had these notice boards outside the Regal saying, "Tonight! Personal Appearance of Veronica Hurst, famous star of *Will Any Gentleman?*" I'd never heard of Veronica Hurst then and wasn't particularly struck by this.

But later on *The Ladykillers* played at the Astoria. Peter Sellers made a personal appearance. He wasn't a big star then - this was the first film that made him a star. I knew him from the *Goon Show* which was the only radio show that I listened to and loved. So I went along and Peter Sellers came on and did a wonderful session entertaining the audience. And then he disappeared and down the side where I was sitting a spotlight hit the exit curtains and he came through with this tray full of ice creams which he was flinging wildly at the audience. I remember one passing right through my fingers into the lap of the man next to me who very generously offered it to me. Sellers went out of the auditorium in this fashion and I rushed out after him. He was giving away signed photographs and I got one from him and thanked him in a Goon voice. And he responded in another Goon voice.

Years later, at the Astoria again, when *Goldfinger* opened they had a personal appearance of Honor Blackman. There was a very elderly manager there who obviously didn't know anything about her background and he introduced her. He should have said she was the famous star of *The Avengers* but he got the title wrong and the whole audience roared with laughter. I was amused to see in an interview only a few years ago Honor Blackman refer to it.

Were these appearances common?

Not that common, but the stars did whip around a few London suburban cinemas promoting their films and it added a bit of sparkle to going to the cinema in Streatham.

The Streatham cinemas were important places as far as their circuits were concerned. We had two really big cinemas. The Gaumont programmes didn't actually play in Streatham until the bombed Gaumont re-opened. You had to go down to the Clifton at Brixton Hill. It was the only cinema that advertised the name of its manager. It always said: "The Clifton Brixton Hill, manager R. A. Brackenridge" - as though this bestowed some great honour. I don't know why his name was there because it was a very seedy place. I remember a day or two after the Gaumont re-opened I went up there after school and picked up a souvenir brochure from the radiator. When I went in shortly after, it had been restyled in a modern manner with a low "floating" ceiling. It was actually a wonderful place to see films. It had been very nicely fitted out but it didn't seem to have big audiences. The only time I ever saw it full was for *Never on Sunday*. The

annoying thing about the Gaumont was that the cheapest seats were just the front three rows. Once I moved back just one row to avoid sitting right at the side and an usherette came all the way down from the back of the cinema, shone a torch on me, and said: "Can I see your ticket, please." I had to move.

Astoria Streatham: 1930 photograph in which can be seen one of the murals alongside the circle

Did you take much notice of the way the interiors of cinemas were decorated?

I think we took them for granted then. You had no reason to suppose they weren't going to be there forever. My art teacher at school asked me what I thought of the panels in the Astoria Streatham and I said, "What do you mean?" These were the Egyptian murals and because I'd always sat in the stalls and they were alongside the circle I'd never seen them. The next time I was there, in the stalls as usual, I remembered what he'd said and I got up and walked down to the front and looked up at the circle and I could see the panels. But then a short while after that, someone came in and revamped the place and all this was whipped out for some more modern look to the building.

But I never really liked the Astoria, it was a very lofty place. It certainly showed lots of good films but I found it a little too old-fashioned in style for my taste. I much preferred the Regal at Streatham which was a building from the later Thirties. It had a proper big CinemaScope screen which was wider than the ordinary one, whereas at the Astoria the masking dropped down, making a smaller picture. The only

Interior of Regal Streatham in 1938

Foyer of Regal Streatham in 1938

thing I didn't like about the Regal was that, as it was an ABC house, like the Rex at Norbury, they were always shoving the ABC Film Review at you. They were monthly magazines which promoted the films coming to ABC cinemas and, of course, never had a bad word to say about them.

Moira Mulholland in the main foyer of the former Astoria Brixton, now the Academy concert hall

Moira Mulholland

Moira Mulholland, born in 1944, currently works for an estate agent and lives in East Dulwich.

Do you remember any films from when you were very young?

One which really sticks in my mind was *Son of Paleface* with Bob Hope and Roy Rogers. And I can really remember going to *The Caine Mutiny* with my mum and dad because my dad fell asleep and my mother was digging him with her elbows to wake him up because he was snoring. That was the Astoria Brixton.

What was it like?

The inside was absolutely lovely. I think I must have spent most of the time just looking round - it was like sitting in a big garden and, as you looked up, there was a house really high with windows all the way around, and trees, and little lights. They were obviously light bulbs but they were meant to look like the stars and the moon, over there behind a tree. It was really pretty, lovely. And, of course, I used to go to Saturday morning pictures there. That was fabulous.

And was it busy at Saturday morning pictures?

Absolutely packed, really packed out. I can remember, when it was your birthday, you got to go up on the stage and I was absolutely astounded to find out, because I looked behind the curtains, that there weren't any Tarzans or lions behind - it was all cables and machinery. And another time I

Congo Bill (1948): Don McGuire (in pith helmet) and Neyle Morrow

went up there, at Saturday morning pictures, was with my yo-yo because Art Pickles, the famous yo-yo man, was showing us how to use our yo-yos, and that was fun.

Were there a lot of staff during children's shows?

They had grown ups but they used to have big boys, young teenagers fourteen years old, walking about keeping an eye on you. The big lads used to keep you in check.

Do you have any memories of the films which were shown on Saturday mornings?

Yes, they had an on-going serial, *Congo Bill.* He used to wear a pith helmet and he was in the jungle, the Congo. He was like a Tarzan with clothes on. And we all used to sing. It used to come up on the screen with a dot. And there would be a big film like *Hue and Cry.*

Did you go with friends?

I used to go with two of the girls up the road and their brother. And then, when I got a bit bigger, I used to take my brother and my sister. But sometimes I used to go on my own. It didn't matter. There were always people there you knew. We'd meet up and congregate and queue up and all go in together.

And you went absolutely regularly?

Every Saturday.

It must have been quite good for parents.

I'm sure it was. My mother used to go into Brixton and do her shopping. That was when they had shops there.

And did you go anywhere else?

When I got a little older, I used to go Sunday afternoons with my friend to the Ritz in Stockwell, opposite Stockwell station. A bit of a fleapit really. And another one was the Empress. They used to have shows there and then they turned it into the Granada. I can remember seeing *Bridge on the River Kwai* there with a girl friend when I was about fourteen. We'd gone in the afternoon and we stayed to see it round again because we met a couple of chaps. We were half-way through the second session of *Bridge on the River Kwai* and this note came up on the screen. It must have been something like half-past eight at night. It had my friend's name on it and it said if she's in the cinema, would she please

"The bee's knees": Lex Barker

go out to the foyer because her parents were there. Boy, she nearly got kicked home - she really got a clip round the ear. I was so glad it wasn't my mum and dad. But they found out because she lived next door to me. I was kept in for six weeks. I never saw the chaps again.

And when you started going out with boys, did you go to the cinema together?

Yes, but all they wanted to do was sit in the back row. It was awful.

Did you have any favourite stars?

I thought Lex Barker was the bee's knees - he was Tarzan for a while. And Rory Calhoun, cowboy extraordinaire - he was nice. And my very favourite of all time was Danny Kaye. I used to see all of his films. Tony Curtis and Marlon Brando and, of course, James Dean. But I think Lex Barker and Rory Calhoun were my favourites because you used to be able to buy pictures of them in the arcades in Brixton. They used to have shops with all pin-up photographs, black-and-white glossy pictures. Then, of course, pop music came along and ruined it. Everybody used to go on records.

Really, you went to cinemas which were in walking distance?

Yes, in Brixton, and the furthest I went was Stockwell.

What was special about the atmosphere in the cinemas?

It makes me think of Woolworth's in Brixton when I was little. It was always a bit like Christmas, sparkly and exciting, and everybody used to behave, which was nice. As soon as the film was on, everyone was really dead quiet and you really used to enjoy it, and at the end of the programme they used to play the anthem up and it really was an event. Even if you did it every week, it was still an occasion.

Tony Sloman at the youth culture exhibit in the Museum of the Moving Image

Tony Sloman

Tony Sloman, born in 1945, works as a film editor and has arranged seasons at the National Film Theatre. His memories are also to be found in Film Talk.

Forest Gate was where I spent the first five years of my life. It had an Odeon right opposite me and probably one of the first things I was taken to see was *Samson and Delilah* at the Odeon Forest Gate - a very sensible film to take a young Jewish boy to see. Most of the films I was taken to see were considered "sensible". *David and Bathsheba* I saw at the Odeon Forest

Gate, which is right in the *Samson and Delilah* tradition. I remember it vividly and being terrified about Gregory Peck with the sackcloth and ashes and the wrath of Jehovah. It was a terrifying experience for a child and I loved and hated it at the same time.

The Greatest Show on Earth was a major experience for me at the Odeon Forest Gate. Most of the films I saw in this period were in Technicolor and I remember the excitement and the romance of the trailers, because I was seeing the trailers for films which were Sunday for one day only, which were like forbidden fruit because I very seldom went on a Sunday. Once I convinced my grandfather to take me to see *The Treasure of the Sierra Madre*.

I loved posters. I remember billboards vividly. I remember even at Forest Gate huge billboards for the Nelson Eddy

Phantom of the Opera. And I remember seeing later huge billboards at the Elephant and Castle, over the bomb sites, for *Captain Horatio Hornblower*, for *Limelight*. And I think that huge billboards were all part of the glamour of going to the movies.

Another thing about Forest Gate was on Sundays sometimes we used to go as a special treat up West - up West was always a big thing - to the newsreel theatres like the Cameo Great Windmill Street where I saw Disney cartoons with my parents, and it was a big thing to go and feed the pigeons in Trafalgar Square and have tea at Lyons and see cartoons in the newsreel theatre.

"A screen full of babies' bottoms":
Kenneth More, Dirk Bogarde, Donald
Sinden, Donald Houston and
unidentified infants in Doctor in the
House

And sometimes, when we were on holiday at Westcliff, I was taken to see films. I remember seeing *Along the Great Divide*, a western with Kirk Douglas. I didn't like it because it was black and white. And a big event: we went to see *Robin Hood,* the Disney Robin Hood, so my first Robin Hood was Richard Todd - it wasn't Errol Flynn's like everyone else's or Kevin Costner's like today's. This is when I terrified my parents because I decided to try out all the different seats in the cinema to figure out which was the best place to sit and they looked round and I wasn't there.

All these were continuous programmes. Expressions like "This is where we came in" were part of my growing up. We got used to seeing things round again to "This is where we came in". It always seemed to me to be a funny way to see things. "You'd never do it with a book", I always used to say to them. "Why do you do it with a film?" But films meant something to me they didn't mean to anyone else. My auntie didn't say it was like going to church but it was something

like that. But I remember my Auntie Doris thought I was very weird. She was right. I was a very selfish child. I was only interested in cinema.

Did you like British films as well as the Hollywood ones?

If there were a choice between British and American films, we always went to see the American films. They were always more exciting, more glamorous. It was really glamour. I didn't know that Continental films existed. I remember there was talk of a film called *The Wages of Fear* and that was French and I also remember my parents getting a babysitter in to go and see *La Ronde*. And again I was annoyed because, whenever they went off and saw something that I couldn't see like this, it used to drive me crazy - it was forbidden fruit time.

Doctor in the House arrived in 1953 at the Astoria Streatham. I wanted to see it and I asked my mother if she'd give me the money and she wouldn't. It was the first time I was refused money to go to the pictures. This was a real challenge and I found a lot of small toys that I didn't want, simple things like playing cards, there were certainly Dinky toys, and I stood outside the house with a hat in Downton Avenue, Streatham, and sold these things in a lucky dip for a penny to anyone who walked past to get my money. This was on a Saturday morning. I don't know, with hindsight you should say people took pity on me, but I certainly sold them. And I remember going in during *Doctor in the House* and walking in at the moment the screen was full of babies' bottoms and they're being powdered and seeing the film round again till that.

Doctor in the House was the first film I remember going to

Doris Day and CinemaScope: Lucky Me *(1954)*

see on my own. I certainly went to see all the 3-D films on my own and I think it was pretty safe then.

And that was roughly the time I realised that adult films were better than Saturday morning pictures, except for one very important Saturday morning at the Regal Streatham and that was when Robby the Robot [from *Forbidden Planet*] visited. He stood outside and he answered questions and he was wonderful. And I have no idea how he answered these questions because they were about things like who won the Cup Final. And I remember being amazed by this, and I went to see *Forbidden Planet* again, loved *Forbidden Planet*. It was a very, very big film for me, one of the key films of my youth. Almost as key for me was *Lucky Me*, almost the same time - "Doris Day, and lucky you, the first musical in CinemaScope", it said on the posters. I had to see it, it was a "U". The bit that I really liked in *Lucky Me* was the bit where Martha Hyer fell into the swimming pool and came out soaking and I thought I could see, if I leaned forward, down the front of her dress. So I had to sit through that bit again. You never could see anything down the front of her dress.

What cinemas did you go to outside Streatham?

The Clifton Brixton Hill was an interesting cinema. They

The Clifton Brixton Hill in its early days as Pyke's Cinematograph Theatre

might have played the circuit release but they used to change the B feature, so I used to see things like a sepia print of *Sun Valley Serenade* on with whatever the A feature was. I do remember seeing *The Yellow Mountain*, when I started scratching and my mother made me take a bath.

The Astoria Tooting was no paradise either. I persuaded my mother to go there to see *A Kid for Two Farthings*. We could have seen it comfortably at the Astoria Streatham on with some British rubbish called *End of the Road* with Finlay Currie. But at the Tooting Astoria it was on with *Burning Arrows* with Anthony Dexter and Jody Lawrence in Cinecolor. So there was no question but I had to drag my poor mum. I was always thinking of the film rather than the inconvenience.

I never really got to see many "A"s because they weren't considered suitable. I remember in school at Streatham there was a girl called Jane Dunn and one evening she had been taken to see *The Lavender Hill Mob* and I was really jealous because I was never taken to the pictures in the evening (it was always called "the pictures"). And also, coming from a Jewish family, we never went out on Friday nights...

The Palladium Brixton, after being modernised, re-opened as the Regal and renamed again the ABC. It is now the Fridge nightclub

Where did you go to school?

I was the first person from my family to go to public school. I was on a scholarship. Coming from an Orthodox family, we had to discuss with my grandfather whether I should go to Dulwich. Dulwich was a six-day school. And he, in his patriarchal wisdom, agreed that yes, I could go to school on Saturday mornings. So, even if I'd wanted to go to Saturday morning pictures, I couldn't. So this put me into Sunday afternoon picture-going. So I saw things like *Silk Stockings* and *H.M.S. Defiant* four o'clock on Sundays.

And there was a thing that my parents never understood. They always said on a really sunny day, "Why do you want to go to the pictures?" And they never understood that it had

<table>
<tr><td colspan="4" align="center">These Programmes are subject to alteration</td></tr>
<tr><td rowspan="2">Sunday Sept. 2 For 7 days</td><td align="center">**ANYTHING GOES** (U)
Colour by Technicolor   In VistaVision</td><td>Bing Crosby
Donald O'Connor
Jeanmaire
Mitzi Gaynor</td></tr>
<tr><td align="center">**Innocents In Paris** (A)</td><td>Alastair Sim
Ronald Shiner</td></tr>
<tr><td rowspan="2">Sunday Sept. 9 For 7 days</td><td align="center">**ROCK AROUND THE CLOCK** (U)
BILL HALEY And His Comets
THE PLATTERS (Ernie Freeman Combo)
TONY MARTINEZ And His Band
FREDDIE BELL And His Bellboys
Alan Freed   Johnny Johnston   Alix Talton</td><td></td></tr>
<tr><td align="center">**ONE GOOD TURN** (U)</td><td>Norman Wisdom</td></tr>
<tr><td rowspan="2">Sunday Sept. 16 For 7 days</td><td align="center">**THE AMBASSADOR'S DAUGHTER** (U)
Print by Technicolor   In CinemaScope</td><td>Olivia de Havilland
John Forsythe
Myrna Loy
Adolphe Menjou</td></tr>
<tr><td align="center">**The Broken Star** (A)</td><td>Howard Duff
Lita Baron
Bill Williams</td></tr>
<tr><td rowspan="2">Sunday Sept. 23 For 7 days</td><td align="center">Ealing Studios Present
THE LONG ARM (U)</td><td>Jack Hawkins</td></tr>
<tr><td align="center">**EDGE OF HELL** (U)</td><td>Hugo Haas</td></tr>
<tr><td rowspan="2">Sunday Sept. 30 For 7 days</td><td align="center">**HE LAUGHED LAST** (U)
Print by Technicolor</td><td>Frankie Laine
Lucy Marlow</td></tr>
<tr><td align="center">**THE LAST MAN TO HANG** (A)</td><td>Tom Conway
Eunice Gayson</td></tr>
<tr><td>Universal News at Every Performance</td><td colspan="2" align="right">Hearing Aids Available Free on Request</td></tr>
</table>

School Outfits (Boys and Girls)
Scoutswear
Guideswear

Agents for: WOLSEY, JAEGER, VANTELLA, VAN HEUSEN, MORLEY, RAEL-BROOK, OLD ENGLAND, MERIDIAN, COOPER'S, CHRISTY, etc. etc. etc.

GAYDON'S OUTFITTERS LTD.
MEN'S AND CHILDREN'S OUTFITTER
91 STREATHAM HILL
Facing Locarno   Tel.: Tulse Hill 6479

"I kind of grew up going there": the Gaumont Streatham programme for September 1956. The building is now a bowling alley

GAUMONT
STREATHAM
Phone: TULse Hill 5251
Manager: J. Kay

★

YOUR FILM ENTERTAINMENT FOR SEPTEMBER

If you miss any of these Programmes and would like to know at which other Odeon or Gaumont Theatre they are showing 'PHONE TRAFALGAR 5471

nothing to do with the weather, or anything. I wanted to go to the pictures because I wanted to go to the pictures.

One little thing about going to school: we walked to the swimming bath. I don't know where it was in Brixton but we walked past a cinema which was being reconstructed and the posters outside had five stars on them and, when the first star came off, an "R" went up. And another star came off and an "E" went up. So every week it was exciting to go swimming because I was going past the

3. TRAD, MODERN and MAINSTREAM

sat, sun, june 3, 4

The fact that British working-class boys in Newcastle play it is at least as interesting as and rather more surprising than the fact that it progressed through the frontier saloons of the Mississippi valley.... At the moment I write this in the spring of 1958 there is probably no major city in the world in which someone is not playing a record of Louis Armstrong or Charlie Parker, or of players influenced by these artists, or improvising on the theme of the *St. Louis Blues* or *Indiana* or *Cherokee*.

Francis Newton,
"The Jazz Scene"

In Person:

The Bruce Turner Jump Band.

Films include:

The first showing of a new British jazz film LIVING JAZZ sponsored by Doug Dobell and Ken Lindsay, directed by Jack Gold.

Note: An L.P. record of the Turner band playing at the National Film Theatre and an E.P. of the music from LIVING JAZZ will be on sale at the theatre.

———————

Acknowledgments

The quotations from musicians come from the book *Hear Me Talkin' to Ya* published by Peter Davies. *The Jazz Scene* was published by MacGibbon and Kee. Films from Warner Bros., United Artists, Contemporary Films, The French Institute, Curzon Films, United States Information Services, Gaumont British, National Telefilm Associates, John King, Time - Life, G.B. Film Library, Columbia Pictures and New Realm. Among the many people who helped with the programme we would like to mention Max Jones of the *Melody Maker*, Jim Godbolt, Roger Mayne, John Kendall, the editorial staff of *Jazz News*, Ernest Smith of New York and Dave Dixon of Vancouver.

The Humphrey Lyttleton Band   Johnny Dankworth

PHOTOS: MELODY MAKER

Six Bells rehearsal: a production still from Living Jazz

PHOTO: BRIAN TUFANO

4   5

Living Jazz *at the National Film Theatre in Summer 1961*

unveiling of what turned out to be the R-E-G-A-L Brixton. And they opened with *Yield to the Night* and I was annoyed it was an "X" and I couldn't go.

I loved quad posters. When I went to Dulwich [College], I'd get a bus from Brixton, then the number 3 from Brixton to Dulwich, and I passed all these wonderful quads outside newsagents, so you would see the change of programme if you were lucky on the way home Thursday - certainly the programme changed on Friday - and you had a whole new batch of posters to look at. And that's even before you

looked them up in The Streatham News.

When I went to Dulwich, I realised I couldn't go to the cinema so frequently, so I persuaded my parents to let me go after school. And the first film I saw after school was *The Long Arm*, a Jack Hawkins crime thing, which was double-billed with a Hugo Haas thing, *Edge of Hell*. That was at the Gaumont Streatham and I kind of grew up going to that cinema. I think it had been bombed in the War. They were rebuilding it and I was there for its first week.

One term my marks were so bad that my parents stopped

me from going to the cinema and I had to lie and say I was at house meetings and things like that.

Did Dulwich College encourage your interest in films?

There was Dulwich and there was movies and, until I was in the fifth and sixth form and I ended up running the film society, they were never really connected. And for the school film society I booked films which I thought people should see which I liked - which is the wrong way to run a film society, as anybody can tell you. So we got *All Quiet on the Western Front* and *Paths of Glory*. I had to do my own posters which were largely based on film ads. They were frowned upon. I just loved *Li'l Abner* and I booked it and nobody went to see it. Nobody ever went to see *Li'l Abner*. So I left Dulwich with the film society in the red, really.

I have good recall. I can't remember anything in life. Both my parents died tragically but I was actually seeking solace in the cinema before I needed to seek solace in the cinema. I didn't know it at the time but my mother was dying and my father was seriously up to no good and I came back from school one day to find something going on and I had no one to turn to. And I had to talk to my form master, Mr. Thornton, but, because he knew I was into movies, he thought I'd kind of made it up, or at least made up half of it. And I hadn't made up any of it. And he said, "You'd better take this afternoon off and go to the pictures." And I saw *Jessica*, with Maurice Chevalier and Angie Dickinson. It wasn't very good. I wasn't really concentrating on it. That, too, was an "X" and had adult themes. I chose that because, when you got off the number 3 bus, it was outside the Granada Brixton and that's what was on at the Granada Brixton.

When did you first watch "art house" films?

I had a wonderful discovery of Bergman in '61 or '62 when the Vogue Tooting ran foreign films. I remember going to see *The Silence* at the Cameo-Royal, which was a major event. I have great gaps in American and British cinema-going of that period because I was only seeing foreign films. It was the time of the Nouvelle Vague, it was '61 through to about '63 when

I was seeing everything as it was coming out. I now wish I'd seen more American stuff of that period, of course.

The first time I went to the National Film Theatre was from Dulwich on a school outing. We were taken to see *Living Jazz*, directed by an unknown called Jack Gold. And when I saw the NFT, that was it. You got programme notes and booklets and it was absolutely fabulous. I was going out with a girl and after school I took her to see *Top Hat*, the first time I went to the NFT on a date. It was just fabulous. She didn't appreciate it. They never did. My whole career is littered with girls who never appreciated what I took them to see.

Did you go to the Trocadero at all?

The Trocadero Elephant and Castle was legendary. It was the biggest cinema - that and the Gaumont State Kilburn. Kilburn was too far for me to ever get near. The Trocadero I used to see from the 133 bus occasionally but I never went there as a cinema because it showed films that were on somewhere else closer. What I went to the Trocadero for, in my delirious teenage period, was the live shows. I saw Bobby Darin, Duane Eddy and Clive McPhatter at the Trocadero and that was fantastic. And I also saw Louis Armstrong, along with Chris Barber (my father made Chris Barber's clothes). For me, the Trocadero was never a cinema. It was where the American stars came.

When you went to the cinema, did you notice the architecture very much?

I didn't notice the interior architecture very much other than the size of the screen. I never understood why, when I went with my parents, they liked sitting upstairs in the balcony which was supposed to be the place to sit. I always liked sitting down in the stalls. You have to remember that if you sit in the front row or close to the front row and look at the screen, you're not too into the architecture. The Granada Tooting was lost on me until they closed it and I realised, "Yes, that was fantastic", and it wasn't there anymore.

Aine O'Halloran outside the former New Victoria cinema, now the Apollo Victoria

Aine O'Halloran

Aine O'Halloran, born in 1950, was part of the Irish community in Pimlico as a child. She usheretted briefly at a Chelsea cinema and now works for the British Film Institute's distribution department. She also appears in Working There.

It was a very big Irish community in Pimlico I came from. Although it was Central London, the Irish Catholics were very isolated. They kept their children very much protected from anybody outside of that network. So there were very rigid allowances of where you could go. So I'm talking about my community.

My first cinema experience was going with my brothers and sisters on Saturday morning. That was the Biograph [Victoria]. The way that the area was structured - it was quite rigid really, the social structure - all kids of eight and around that age went Saturday mornings to the Biograph. And kids that were slightly better off than some of us went up to the Gaumont in King's Road which is like ten minutes the other way.

All I can remember about the Biograph is Daisy who worked in the box-office. Daisy was quite old even then - which would be about 1958 - so my brother, who was really tall, went up first and paid his entrance fee while we all skipped in underneath the actual box-office so she didn't see us and we had some money for lollies. But I don't remember anyone really actually watching the pictures, apart from *Zorro*. That kept them quiet. Mostly we threw the lollies at each other. That was about it.

And did you start going regularly, every Saturday?

Oh, yes. It was used as a creche really. On Saturday mornings your mother kicked you out and you'd go to the pictures - it kept you out of her hair whilst she got on with things like shopping and getting stuff ready for Monday.

Were you aware of what the building was like?

Not really. I can just remember it being very dark and always thinking they're going to come and catch us for not having paid.

But not many of the films stand out?

Not really, apart from *Zorro*, because we all wanted to save up to have a cape and a plastic sword with a bit of chalk on the end.

So how old were you when you started going to the pictures in the evenings?

I would have been eighteen before I was allowed to go in the evenings. There was a structure. From eight, maybe up to ten, you did the Biograph. Your big brothers were going to the New Vic, which was the big one, on the Sunday afternoon. Everybody in the community went to the cinema on the Sunday afternoon. All the teenagers went to the New Vic, because that was where you met your partner for life, that was the network.

So you would go through the Biograph waiting for the day when you would be old enough to go to the New Vic - which was around fourteen. But it was a Sunday afternoon - it wasn't the evening. The evenings weren't something you did until you went to work much later on.

The Wilton Road frontage of the New Victoria in 1977

The stage between the Biograph and the New Vic was the News Theatre. It was slightly more expensive but you could stay there all day because it just kept going round. So twelvish, when you were really desperate to go to the New

The former News Theatre in Victoria Station as the Cartoon Theatre in 1977

Vic on Sunday afternoon, you'd feel slightly more grown up because you went to the News Theatre Saturday afternoon.

When you moved into the fourteen/fifteen bracket, it was really a lot of money because it was three shillings-and-sixpence at the New Vic. And again we found the way in: somebody would pay to get in and then let you in through the side door on Vauxhall Bridge Road which actually took you to the gents toilet. So for years when I first started going to that cinema I always found myself sitting in the very front row because that was the only one you could get to before the usherette would catch you once you came out of the gents. It took me a very long time to realise that you could actually go back once you paid.

Was everybody trying to bunk in?

Of course. There was no money, because there were huge Catholic families, so you did every scam you could possibly find of not actually paying to go to the cinema.

But you would not admit that to your parents?

No. They would be devastated if they thought we were doing things like that.

What about the other cinemas at Victoria?

The only cinema which was banned was the Cameo. I don't know why because I never ever trod foot in it. My mother always used the phrase "blue films" but whether it did or not I don't know. We just used to scurry past it, look at the Metropole. Later on, as the next end of the family started growing up, the Biograph became less of a place that you would let anyone go. My mother wouldn't have been happy for them to go to the Biograph because the whole clientele had changed so dramatically in a short number of years.

You mentioned the Metropole. How did that rate?

Nobody could afford to go to the Metropole. If some really rich bloke asked you out, you would say the New Vic and he'd pay for you; but if he'd said the Metropole you would have blown him out because he was out of your league entirely.

Did you start developing favourite films, favourite stars?

No. Cinema-going was totally to do with where you were, at what stage of your life. Up until I was, probably, sixteen, the whole cinema experience was to do with being with a group of people. At the New Vic, the film changed on Sunday and you watched whatever was coming on. When a James Bond film would come, there would be hundreds of thousands of people who shouldn't really have been there, because they were blow ins, they weren't locals at all. So there would be huge queues. I was much older when I started to think about what I was going to see and why I was going to see it.

And when you were about fourteen/fifteen, would you sometimes go with a group of girls?

Always. The thing was the lads came in and the girls came in and you'd see them over there, usually about half a dozen, and you'd hope they'd come over and talk to you. Everyone would get in really early, before the film, so you could be seen flitting around and you could shout over at folk. It was a social gathering rather than a visit to the cinema as such.

So the group of girls that you went with would be from the Catholic community?

Yes, rather than schoolmates, they would actually be the people who lived around me. I went to a mixed secondary school, a non-Catholic secondary school. Schoolmates didn't really live around me because all the Irish were in enclaves.

What was the New Vic like?

The New Vic was really clean. It was vast compared to the Biograph and then the News Theatre, which was where I'd been. It was really big. I was sitting up there thinking one day, if you fell off this balcony you'd die, you'd definitely die. My memory of it is that it was a really comfortable cinema. You could see everybody.

"Really clean, really big": inside the New Victoria in 1971

Did you go upstairs when it was a particularly good film?

No, when some bloke asked to take me. I never paid four-and-six myself. No, oh Lord, no.

If you were asked out, it would always be to the cinema?

Yes. There was nowhere else to go. You couldn't go to pubs, and things like youth clubs hadn't really begun in that way apart from like the Methodist ping-pong club which nobody in their right mind would go to. So if anybody asked you out,

they asked you out on Sunday and then their mates could see that they had got a girl they were meeting. It was all part of the whole thing.

And did you get up to anything?

Yes, sometimes I sucked his lolly. No. I don't know what other communities were like but we were very rigidly brought up as Catholics and so you would have a good snog but that would be it.

And you would sit away from the main group?

Of course you did. The back row. But you'd make sure they all saw. Each of the groups had to see that you'd pulled. But you would then go and sit on your own. The big deal was if you came up in a love bite Monday morning - a status symbol.

So you don't remember any of the films particularly?

Absolutely not. I can remember seeing *Georgy Girl*. I can't think of another film I ever saw on Sunday afternoon.

Did you still go to the Victoria cinemas later on?

When my son was three, some friends were going to see *Bugsy Malone* at the Metropole and said did I want to go. I didn't have a baby sitter, so I thought I'll try, I'll take him with me and if he really plays up, I'll go home. I can remember going into the Metropole for the first time in my life, and at that stage I'm twenty-five or twenty-eight, thinking "Christ, I shouldn't be here - they'll find out I'm poor and throw me out". I was sitting with Patrick and he sat absolutely entranced through the whole movie and has been like that ever since with cinema. He has videos and he watches TV but there is nothing like the cinema experience for my son, which I think is really great. That was my one and only trip to the Metropole. I remember thinking, why was it so expensive - it was fifteen shillings or something and we were paying three-and-six and four-and-six at the New Vic, so it was three times as much. But it was a real good investment because my son is such an enthusiast of the cinema.

And, towards the end of its life, the Biograph had a really good programming policy and you could see great double bills for next to nothing. I saw *Little Big Man* and I forget what it was double-billed with - but with a really good film. But it was a gay haunt and because it was so close to Victoria Station, as a lot of the benches and stuff were closed down, a lot of the winos who used to hang around the station would move up. The cinema was so close that for a very small amount of money they could sit happily all day in the warmth out of the rain. So you either had a very smelly tramp rustling newspapers around him or really quite a sleazy gay haunt, not a pleasant one.

You had to put up with the lights being half on, which is what they did, and with the extraordinary complete movement all around you and then a tramp would wake up and rustle. So unless you could really concentrate on the movie, it wasn't worth the effort. It was an unpleasant and uncomfortable experience. And this same poor old Daisy was still in the box-office and she would say to women as they went to the loo, "You don't want to go in there, dear. It's not very nice."

But it was the last of them. The Biograph outlasted everything else. The New Vic had become a stage show place by then. The Metropole became a nightclub. The Cameo was Dickie Dirts for a while, selling jeans. And the News Theatre closed down a long time before that.

The Biograph outlasted the rest - but succumbed to sudden demolition in August 1983

Working There

These interviews focus on the experience of working in cinemas. For most, it started as just a job, although in one instance a fascination with how films reached the screen led to a desire to be part of the process.

In the Thirties, youngsters started at fourteen as page boys helping the doormen control the queues and running errands. If they were bright and lucky, page boys gained the chance to work in the projection room where they learned the routines. Joining as a fourth projectionist meant polishing floors and brasswork: it could take months to be allowed to handle the projectors and reels of film. Highly inflammable nitrate film was used until the early Fifties and the projectors could never be left unattended. Two projectors were needed, each showing twenty minute reels in turn, with the handling of the change-over (timed by dots in the right hand corner at the ends of reels) being one of the projectionist's most skilled chores, along with adjusting the carbon arcs that provided the illumination of the image. It is a far cry from today's automated projection suites with their single projectors and complete programmes on "cakestands" or "towers".

This was a highly isolated world, so far from street level that in many of the large super cinemas projection staff rarely descended from their portholed eerie during the working day. At one time, 66-hour weeks were worked with very limited time off, and with (it seems) the chief always bagging Saturday evening for himself. Projectionists found companionship in their time off with usherettes who worked the same awkward hours, and love affairs and marriages resulted.

Usherettes had to tear tickets in half, returning one half and filing the other half on a string, and show patrons to their seats. Many picturegoers arrived in the middle of a film (shows were continuous performances) and needed guiding in the dark, and they had to be seated in the section for which they had paid (there would usually be three different prices for seats in the stalls, the cheapest seats being at the front; and at least two prices for circle seats). Usherettes had to keep an eye on how many seats were unoccupied at busy periods and during full houses fill seats with patrons standing at the back or sides as people left, besides keeping an eye open for children sneaking in by the side exits without paying. Some usherettes would load the icecream trays and stand under a spotlight at the intervals dispensing to the eager queues. Large cinemas would have four or more girls selling ice-cream during the intervals.

Better paid than usherettes were the cashiers who took the money and checked as best they could that kids were properly accompanied to "A" films and young enough to qualify for children's prices. The managers were top of the staffing hierarchy. The manager of a super cinema had a place in the community equivalent to a bank manager, and part of his role would be to appear in the foyer in evening dress and greet patrons arriving for the evening performance. Women managers were very few, and women projectionists even more scarce except during the War years when they were deliberately recruited to ease the staffing shortage.

Circuit cinema managers tended to move around the country as vacancies occurred and they gained promotion to higher grades. Those working in the big South London cinemas in the Fifties tended to be quite elderly, as promotion to managing these important halls often came late in their careers. This partly explains why we have not located any managers to contribute to this section.

Sid Cove

Sid Cove, born in 1917, was a cinema projectionist who became a cabinet maker. He has built an intricate model of a cinema which remains a prize possession in his flat near the Oval. His reminiscences also appear in Being There.

During the early Thirties there was plenty of unemployment. If you got a job straight from school you were very lucky. I applied at the Tower Cinema, Rye Lane. They were making enquiries for page boys at this new cinema opening in Peckham, the Gaumont Palace. So I applied for the job and one thing which helped me was my size. I was very small. And three page boys they were after and three of us got picked. I went up to this Tower Cinema, got measured for my uniform and started a week before the opening of the Gaumont Palace Peckham, February 8th 1932.

Did you go for that job because you were already interested in cinema?

No. I knew nothing about cinema. In those days, your parents wanted you to get a job because unemployment was very bad. So if you got a position, a job, it was very good to start off with - you weren't just running the streets. I left school at Christmas and I started in February at this cinema. I knew nothing about the cinema but I was greatly interested once I got the position.

Can you describe the opening of the Gaumont Palace?

It was opened by the Mayor of Camberwell - I think Pearman was the Mayor - and it was a full spread in the Daily Sketch, which doesn't exist today. The Daily Sketch showed a full page the next day of the opening. It was a big thing in those days because things were pretty quiet and that happening in Peckham was great. Now I think the film was *Hindle Wakes* and Sydney Howard in *The Calendar*. We used

to have a stage show which comprised of two or three acts, an orchestra and an organ show - so for sixpence, which it was in those days, it was quite a day out or evening out. And there used to be three complete programmes a day.

How big was the Gaumont Palace?

The Gaumont Palace Peckham seated 2,120 approximately. And you could say most evenings that was full up. The front stalls were about sixpence, then it was one shilling and one shilling-and-threepence; and one shilling-and-threepence upstairs.

The Gaumont Palace Peckham in 1932: exterior

What exactly did a page boy do?

We used to run around for the stage artistes. We used to go to the local ABC restaurant - they don't exist today - and get their teas. Or run messages for the manager, and then again if there was any synopsis or film programmes wanted for forthcoming events, we used to go to Wardour Street, which was the centre of the film industry, and pick up all the synopses and programmes for the next two or three weeks. We were really general messengers. Then help on the front controlling the queues, helping the people in and directing them to the circle, stalls, or wherever it may be. And just made ourselves generally useful. We used to start about ten o'clock. We did a full day really, ten till nine, and then we were away. It was a very long day. But I was young and it wasn't very hard work. And, being in the cinema, you used to get in now and again and watch the films if you could. But your job was the front so you weren't free to sit. Now the usherettes and the attendants, they could see the programmes through and perhaps get fed up with them, but we used to sneak in now and again, especially if there were any good films on.

What did you do with the variety acts when you were a page boy?

The Gaumont Palace Peckham in 1932: entrance hall

When I was at Peckham, it was such a small stage that nothing was on the stage. The stage was empty. Once the film had finished, the curtains would close and the organist would come and play ten minutes. While that was going on, we were all working like mad. We used to put all the seats on for the band, all the band instruments used to go on. It was all got ready. Then when the organist finished his bit, I'd get my card and have the name of the artist or band or whatever and I used to walk on the stage, all smart. The spotlight would come on. On one occasion, there was a little girl who used to live in the flat upstairs and she shouted out, "Mum, there's Sid!" That was one of my little jobs, three times a week, all for ten bob a week.

Can you tell me about the bands in cinemas?

One period, about 1933, when we weren't having the acts we used to have a different band every week. We'd get a saxophone band, an accordion band, a ladies' band. Bobby Howe and His Band, that was a very popular band.

What was your uniform?

We used to have a peak cap, gloves in the lapel, with about twenty little brass buttons right down the tunic. And gloves on the shoulder, buttoned right up to the neck. That was the uniform. I think we had a tunic and two pairs of trousers and a peaked cap. But the usherettes' uniforms were much better. In those days there were three circuits: there were the Gaumonts, the Odeons and the Paramounts and they were all very competitive in their style of uniform. Paramount, an American firm, laid out more money and they used to dress them very smart, like mannequins. But Gaumont, it was all red dresses with just little press studs down the front. They were all right. The same with the men's uniforms. Paramount's were more stylish, brown with gold. Now with Gaumont, they were just gold epaulettes and blue, the same as the page boy's uniform really.

Who was your immediate boss? Did you use to report to the commissionaires?

Our head man was Mr. Lewis. He was the head attendant. We'd report to him every morning and he'd give us our jobs

The Gaumont Palace Peckham in 1932: auditorium

for the day or had us standing there. We had a standing position on the front - we'd stand there, one or two, until we were called away for a message to be run somewhere for somebody. There were three of us. And I was made the sergeant. It was an enjoyable job. There was always something happening.

What did you have to do with the queue?

The doorman was the main chappie controlling the queues, but we just used to have to go along the queues saying how long they might have to wait. If it was pouring with rain, they had canopies outside, but they used to try to bring them in if they could, if they could push them inside. But the LCC [London County Council] wouldn't let you have too many people in the building. Our job as page boys was to tell them where to go, direct them to certain parts of the theatre and let them have standing room in the theatre. The LCC was very strict - a manager could lose his licence if he had too many standing in the building, in case of fire, because film was inflammable then

It was nitrate film.

That's right. Now they've got the great big spools. In my day they only had about 1,000 feet on a spool because if that caught light there was only 1,000 feet to burn and they could perhaps put asbestos sheeting over it and smother it away. You always had two men on duty. One was feeding the machine and the other one was showing the film.

Did you get attracted to projection while you were at the Gaumont?

Well, there's no future in being a page boy except possibly to become an attendant or doorman or something like that which is not much of a future. You're not learning... It was a job but it wasn't much for a youngster. What they did was that when you got past the age of sixteen, and if you were intelligent

Line up of Gaumont circuit programmes in central South London for May 1939

enough, they asked you if you'd like to go in the projection room. But don't forget that, when you go into the projection room, you know you're going to tie yourself down. Now my teenage years were all work, when you work it out. I used to leave home about half-past nine, get there at ten or half-past, and I was on then till eleven o'clock at night. So you tied yourself down to the cinema. I've never been a big football enthusiast because I could never go with my mates. When I got promoted to the projection room, that was a lot of work. What happened was the manager said, "Would you like to go in the box?" Of a night he used to let me go in the box to learn the ropes, just rewind the films and see how it all worked. For about a month I used to go up an hour, a couple of hours, to see how it all worked. And then a vacancy came along at the Canterbury, Westminster Bridge Road, just opposite The Cut. That was a very old theatre. When you went backstage, it smelled musty. Marie Lloyd and all the oldies had been there evidently. It got bombed in the War and got destroyed. All that is left now is an archway. It's boarded up.

Was that owned by Gaumont?

Yes. Gaumont owned quite a few hundred. They'd taken over all the small places, all the independents.

Can you describe the Canterbury?

From Westminster Bridge Road you had a very long entrance, the reason being that Waterloo Station ran right over the entrance hall at the

Canterbury. So you had to walk through lots of archways, like going through a subway, quite a long walk. On either side, you had all the billings advertising programmes coming. It just went on and on. When you got to the end, the arches disappeared and you came into the main theatre itself. The projection room was fixed up at the back of the stalls in what used to be the old gents' toilet, because the other side was the ladies which still existed at the time. The thing about that still had boxes there, the side boxes from the music hall. But we used one of the side boxes for playing the music during the intervals. They had what they called a non-sync. They didn't have an organ there so they used to play music to fill up before the stage came on. And that was one of my jobs, being the rewind boy. I used to go there and play records during the interval. In those days you couldn't put the music equipment for playing records in the projection room because

The Canterbury Westminster Bridge Road when it was a music hall

was: if anybody was a bit tall, they'd cut the picture off when they were walking by the screen. They put it as high as they could because of hitting the circle ceiling. It was a very old place.

Was the decoration pretty?

It was. It could have done with a coat of paint. And they it was inflammable. Anything which was inflammable couldn't be kept in the projection room - only the film, which was highly deadly.

And then, when I started as a projectionist, as a junior, I used to assist on the stage with the spotlights. On one particular occasion, we had a stage show there. The stage show was on. The chief projectionist or the second projectionist used to work the stage lights for the turns, floodlights and all the automatic lights. And on one occasion he pulled the wrong chain and it flooded all the orchestra pit. In the case of fire, they had water valves so you had a safety curtain which used to be raised up and down every programme and the next one was a water drencher. The water up there got to come down to put the fire out and he pulled that. I was on the side. The water was concentrated on the front of the stage so on the side you were pretty safe. But they had to get the electrics switched off because of the water and all the dye came out of the curtains. Another bloke might have got the sack but he was a friend of the circuit manager.

It was a vast stage at the Canterbury. They used to have two spotlights. There wasn't a big stage show. It comprised of about two artists and an orchestra, and they used to play there three times a day. When we'd finished the stage show, we'd go back to the projection room and there used to be two films, a newsreel, and the stage show, so you got your money's worth in those days as regards entertainment.

Was the orchestra a resident orchestra?

Yes. It was what they called a pit band. They didn't do much stage work. They were solely for the orchestra pit, comprised about six bandsmen, and they were permanent, resident.

The variety acts changed every week?

That's right.

Did you have any big names?

In those days the cinema never had the big names because they couldn't afford to pay the very big. But they had those who were up and coming. Ted Ray, he was there, and Alfredo Campoli - he was a famous violinist. Then we had Morris and Cowley - that was a double act: one was a pianist and the other used to crack jokes. Only two acts each week.

How long were you at the Canterbury?

I stayed there about two years. Being the rewind boy, junior projectionist, you used to collect the films. The film transport used to come every night every time there was a change. In our case, at the Canterbury, it was a Wednesday night, a Saturday night and a Sunday night. They used to drop off the new films and pick up the old ones. And a film in those days comprised of about eight, nine or ten reels, and to carry them was heavy. They used to be in a kit bag.

You could wheel them?

I thought of that as I've grown older. If only I could have had an old pram, a box cart, anything. As I told you, we had that long walk along the archway to the theatre. A film had to be got ready for projection. If there were ten reels, you would put two together. You had a morning's work preparing them. Then you had to get the inserts for trailers. At the end of the film you'd have a trailer put on, "Showing next week", and insert all the bits and pieces, what stage show you'd got and what band you'd got coming. All that had to be made up each week for the following week. In the mornings you used to go round cleaning all the lights. We used to have a rota for going round the staircases, the exits, the chandeliers - you used to have to get them down, spend about an hour cleaning all the glass, changing the bulbs as they blew. That was my first two years in the projection room.

When you said the Canterbury was a little bit shabby...

It had been neglected.

Was it a bit more down market place to go? Cheaper?

Yes. It had seen the best of its days.

So when did you leave there?

I got transferred. Gaumonts was a big circuit. They had six or seven in the West End. I was transferred to the Marble Arch Pavilion. That was a leg up, a fourth operator, but it wasn't so hectic as the Canterbury. The Marble Arch Pavilion was solely films - just one film and a newsreel. It was only about a thousand seater if that, but it was a prestige West End cinema in those days and it showed all the first run films as they came out.

I didn't get on very well with the chief there. In those days they had two projectors, left and right. When you ran a film you had a reel on this projector and you'd get the other one ready because there's a change-over. Today you have these great big reels and they put a whole programme on one projector. In those days, you had about twenty minutes on each projector. When it got to the end of the reel, a little dot came up on the top right-hand corner. Well, we wouldn't be looking all the time and, when the reel gets that low, a bell rings. That's the cue - you light the arc lamp up, prepare it, operator stands by, he's ready. When it's getting near, you'd look how far you'd got and then you'd look on the screen, top right-hand corner, because there's a little dot. It's done on the film with four little bits of paint put on, those little dots are on four frames. If you missed it, you got a blank white screen. You remind the bloke because you can easily miss it: "Motor up." When you say "motor", you switch on, start that machine up and you're off onto the next machine. The first machine then has to be laced up, re-carbonned. We had carbons in those days, you didn't have bulbs, and they'd burn out - you had to re-charge them. I'm on the short side and I could never really reach up properly. I believe he got me transferred. He said this bloke isn't really big enough for this job and when you do a bad change-over you're getting a blank screen. I might cut this one off too quick or open that one too early, or they might both be late, and that's terrible, especially in the West End. Anyway, I lasted there a year, possibly not as long as that.

Then I got transferred to the Tivoli in the Strand. That was a super place. That had the stalls, grand circle and a gallery. I enjoyed it there. I think I was there as fourth operator. There were about five operators there at the time. The chief, second, third, fourth and fifth.

What would be the difference?

The fifth is the rewind boy, the general runabout. The fourth is a little bit higher, another grade up, a bit more money in your pocket.

You'd do the change-overs?

Yes, you can go on the machine. When you're a third, you control it. You've learned enough to know how it works. You start the machine at the right time, then you press your curtains, you press your house lights to go down, the curtains open, you turn your sound up. You have it all synchronised together. But as a junior you wouldn't touch that. You'd stand by the machine if he wanted to go to the toilet for a few minutes, but you wouldn't do any of the operating or the changing over.

The Tivoli Strand circa 1946

While you were working in the West End, did you travel up every day?

I always cycled, everywhere I went. I cycled from Peckham to the Strand. And I was coming home one night and a motor car came round Villiers Street and he knocked me off my bike. Charing Cross Hospital was open then, just off the Strand, and they done me up. I'd broken a couple of fingers. So I was out of work for six weeks. During my sickness, there was a cinema strike. The projectionists were out on strike for more money. So they had a three or four weeks' strike. As I wasn't involved in the strike, I went back to work. They lost their jobs but as I was sick and I was genuine, I got back to the Tivoli again.

What was the union the projectionists belonged to?

The ETU, Electrical Trade Union. I was in the union. If I hadn't been sick, I would have been on strike with them. I think eventually they all got their jobs back. After the strike, everything was a little bit upside down and there was a lot of changing the projectionists around the Gaumont cinemas. So I was promoted to a third projectionist and then they said, "Would you like the third projectionist's job at the New Cross Kinema. We want a chappie up there and it will be nearer home for you." I said yes.

The New Cross Kinema was one of the supers of the day. They had an organ and when I got there it wasn't being used regular. They were used every week because they were an attraction, but after a while people got fed up with the organ and used to use that time during the interval for going to the toilets or buying an ice cream or meeting friends and having a chat. The organ wasn't used so much. They kept the organs on site but they weren't using them.

"One of the supers of the day": the New Cross Kinema circa 1946

I went there as third projectionist. Nice little crowd, nice little box, not very big, but we had a decent staff with us. It was just two films and a newsreel, possibly a *March of Time* which was a news effort they put out now and again. And I spent about two years there as a projectionist.

What happened in the War during air raids?

We used to go into the basement in case of air raids. But as time went by, we used to show a slide on the screen - "Air raid now in progress - if you wish to leave the building you may do so, but we will continue showing the programme".

They let people decide for themselves what they were going to do.

I got called up and when I came back after the War I reported back to Gaumonts and they employed me at the King's Cross Cinema as a second projectionist and I stopped there for a period of two years. There were no stage shows then. It was solely films.

Is that when stage shows vanished? During the war?

No, prior to the War, about '36. They started off in '32 and they were very popular but they fizzled out about 1936 because they were losing a lot of money.

When did you go to the Trocadero?

I went there about '48 or '49.

Was that promotion?

Yes, I was a second. I went as co-chief there. I wasn't a chief. I was just one below the chief. And it was a big responsibility there, because it was a big place. Stage shows had fizzled out. They used to have an organ show, a regular organ show every week. And it had a projection room to be proud of. It was a great big room: it had three cinema projectors; a Brenograph, which was an effects machine; two spotlights; and it had recording apparatus. That was a very up-to-date projection room at the Troc. I was there for about two years.

When did you do the effects with the Brenograph machine? Before the programme started?

On the opening of the film sometimes or during an organ interlude. Quentin Maclean wasn't there when I was there. He was one of the most famous organists. He started at the Regal Marble Arch and then he got transferred to the Troc and that's where he made his name. And he broadcast from there. Everybody in the trade knew Quentin Maclean. He was the biz.

Stan Place was the chief projectionist at the Troc and had been for a few years. He knew his equipment. He knew how to put a slide on and make it effective. He'd have the programme Maclean was going to play next week on his organ and they'd have a little chat in the pub. He'd say, "I'm going to do all about Father Thames", and he'd do everything

In a normal theatre, they just put an organ on and play, play, play. But there you'd have the words come up. I used to work the words. That could get you messed up. Something went wrong one Saturday night. I used to have a stack of slides like that, and you'd put them through the projector. We had a speaker in the box so you could hear what he was playing. They're singing like mad down there. Take that one out, put it there, get the next one, put that in... when it

The huge auditorium of the Trocadero (1930 photograph)

to do with Father Thames, all the bridges, everything to fit in with the music. Or, if it was about the sea or weather or autumn, he'd get this Brenograph out and he had rows and rows of slides. They must have laid the money out - anything you wanted, they had it and he'd put it on.

comes to the end of the chorus, or whatever the song is, fade it out, then the other one, open, out, in, out, in. Something happened once, someone wanted help, a lot of things happening in the projection room. I was trying to help him. I lost it. I didn't know where I was. All right, I put another in,

*Rear circle and projection portholes of the Trocadero Elephant
and Castle, photographed in 1930*

flicked it shut. I didn't have any idea where I was. I had half
my slides there and I couldn't use them. The manager came
up. I think he accepted it. He thought a junior was on it and
done it all wrong. So he looked at me. He thought, "Sid
wouldn't muck it up", something had to be wrong. I
apologised to the organist. He was down there playing away.
Well, I couldn't find it. You don't have time to find out
where it is. He played his tunes but he didn't have a slide to
back him up. That's when I came out of the cinema and done
another job, done a bit of cabinet making. That was it.

**During your time at the Trocadero, did you
notice a decline in the audience?**

Oh yes. The Trocadero was about 3,500 and in the
afternoons you'd come through the circle, you'd see a sea of
empty seats. There wasn't a soul in sight. Even the weekend,
which was the best for getting the crowds, you could look in
the cinema and see not many seats were occupied, just rows
and rows of empty seats. Then the word went round they
were talking about closing it. Never. They thought they'd
find another use for it, turn it to a more theatrical use. But it
didn't work out that way. It went on till the beginning of the
Sixties. They demolished it and built a small thousand-seater
Odeon on the site.

Albert Critoph on Waterloo Station. Behind him, where the entrance to the News Theatre used to be

Albert Critoph

———————

Albert Critoph, born in 1922, moved from projecting in cinemas to similar work in a film studio. He is an honorary member of the British Kinematograph Society.

I was interested in the film industry from about seven years of age. I used to get a cardboard box and an egg cup and cut a hole on the inside of the box and, with a little bull's eye torch, project a light on the wall. At Christmas time my father bought me a torch arrangement with a lens attachment. You could take it off and use it for slides, and the slides were small - about four pictures in a circle, cartoons and things - and that was my first start. Another Christmas present a few years later was a Bingascope - this was a film projector and you had about ninety foot of 35mm film and you had a little spool, you'd thread up the projector and you turned a handle.

When I was going to the cinema when I was very, very young, I was always looking up towards the projection room and I saw the changeovers and I more or less had a knowledgeable idea of what was going on. I felt I could go in there and work it. The only thing that I thought then was, when the films were running through the projector, I thought that to get sound there was a gramophone needle on the film. That was the idea in my mind.

I went to this particular cinema, the Savoy in York Road, Battersea, and there they had the screen tabs and main tabs

The Waterloo Station News Theatre in 1934

and I always wanted to see that screen. I'd have loved to go up on stage and see that screen. I'd love to have seen that screen open.

Then, when I went to a cinema, there was often a sign that said "Sound system leased from Western Electric". I didn't know what "lease" actually meant and I always thought there were wires and things from a central point to every cinema and that the system couldn't run except from this main base in London. I thought that was where the sound system was from, not actually from the picture.

When I was fourteen, they said to me at school, "What type of job do you want?" and they'd help you get employment. I said, "I would like to work in a projection room." And they were flabbergasted. So my father's brother was a taxi driver and he helped me a lot. In those days you couldn't start in the projection room. You had to start front of house as a page boy. I believe my uncle found out about a job from a labour exchange in the West End at this news

theatre, the Cameo in Charing Cross Road. So I went along and had an interview and started as a page boy.

What were your duties?

You were more or less like a messenger really, and you had to stand in front of the cinema calling out the prices of the seats. They had other cinemas around the West End and I used to take the accounts, the takings, to head office in Piccadilly. There were three cinema page boys and I was getting fifteen shillings a week.

Albert Critoph as a page boy

What were the working hours?

I was only allowed to do so many hours. Of course, news

theatres opened at ten o'clock in the morning, so one week I would do nine o'clock to seven o'clock and the following week two o'clock to nine thirty. And while I was there I had time off to go to evening class and swot up on electrics. They asked me to do that. Obviously, if you're going to be a projectionist, you had to do a certain amount of electrics anyway. In the smaller cinemas, you helped do some of the wiring.

So how did your career progress?

Later on they made me the head page boy and I got seventeen [shillings] and six[pence], another half-a-crown. I always wanted to go up to the projection room - it was like getting into Buckingham Palace. Then I had a chance to go round to this other cinema, the Centre News Cinema opposite the Windmill Theatre, and start as a rewind boy and I went up another half-a-crown or something. And that's where I started my projection career. This was 1936. When you're a youngster, you're inclined to rewind the reels very, very fast, but you always had somebody to give you a nudge on the shoulder to rewind very slowly and check for joins, this, that, and the other.

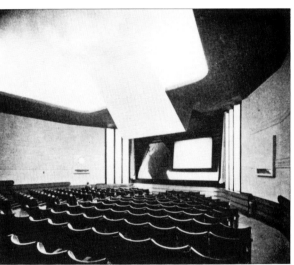

The Waterloo Station News Theatre: interior 1934

What did you do when you weren't rewinding?

You'd just stand by the machine. Or the projectionists loved their jugs of tea and you'd go across the road and get their jugs of tea. And cleaning - in projection rooms in those days there was a lot of brasswork about and you were always kept busy cleaning the brass.

The Cameo was like the flagship of newsreel theatres, although it was only a single tier. They cut their news together. You had two or three newsreels and obviously they carried more or less the same items and we'd project them in the morning for the manager and cut out the best material and put all the news into one. The programmes were only an hour and what they used to do sometimes with the comedy type of films we had was they'd take one bit of one comedy film and another bit of another comedy film and they were edited together and they used to call it "Crazy Week".

I can remember, if you took *The March of Time* back on the Saturday night on time to Dispatch in Soho Square at RKO Radio so that someone else could have the copy, they gave you a shilling. The Walt Disney cartoons went back to the same place but it was the *March of Time* that if you took it back on time they gave you a shilling.

How often did you get Saturday night off?

You try and wangle a Saturday night off! It was like gold dust. The chap who used to get Saturday night off was the chief projectionist.

Did the projection staff mix with the usherettes and other staff downstairs?

For some reason or other, the usherettes always looked up to the projectionists. You went into the cinema at half-past ten and didn't finish until eleven o'clock at night. You had one so-called early night, either seven o'clock or nine o'clock, and you got one night off a week. Some cinemas you never even got a Sunday off and some places they had one Sunday off in three. Often there were love affairs between the usherettes and the projectionists, and often you'd find an usherette would work a day off with you.

You worked in the station news theatres.

I went on to Classics and they had two news theatres in the stations, at Victoria and Waterloo. We used to get our electricity supply from the railways and during the War the cinemas closed quite a lot with the bombs dropping and the electricity supply [being cut off]. The clocks in the cinemas were coupled up with those on the platforms as well. You kept patrons informed of arrivals and departures. We used to write out a glass slide and use a slide projector to put it on a small screen, a bit of plaster with some moulding around it no more than three or four feet square alongside the sound screen. And you would scribble out "So and so boat train delayed"... The slide projector at Victoria was in the projection room but the one at Waterloo was down an iron staircase and they had a little room there with the slide projector and the cap to cut the picture off was the lid of a Cherry Blossom boot polish tin.

How many operators were there?

Usually about four or five. In those days you had to have quite a number of staff because of the nitrate film. The projectionist couldn't be left on his own. When I was a rewind boy I was never allowed to be left on my own.

How was it you came to move to a large cinema like the Metropole at Victoria?

Peter Jackson, the chief projectionist, knew me before I went there. A friend of mine was working there. He went into the Forces. I took his job and, when I got my first week's salary, I said to Peter, "I think I've been overpaid." "Oh, no," he said, "They've had a good week."

Presumably that was very rare.

Oh yes, very rare. Practically every week you had extra money. The Hyams brothers were so good. They also owned the cinema round the corner in Wilton Road, the Biograph. I was told the money from that cinema, the Biograph, paid to have the Metropole built. We used to cross over the news - we had just one print. I used to go down and pick up the news.

Queues outside the Metropole Victoria for Lost Horizon *in 1937*

The Metropole, they'd run a new programme on a Sunday, run through to Saturday night. We always had a rehearsal. We had the prints two or three days beforehand. At the Metropole you always had two big features on together in one show and they called it a pre-release from the West End. What happened was, you had these two big films on a very long programme. The following week the films would go on release and one feature would go to one cinema and the other to another. But we had it on one programme. In those days, when it went from the Metropole, it went north of the Thames, then the following week the programmes would come over the Thames to the south.

Most cinemas have only got two projectors but the Metropole had three projectors. They'd switch them around but sometimes the third projector would be just used for the news only. And we also had a Brenograph machine. That's a double lantern arrangement. You could fade one slide out and bring the other one in. And you could put bits of frosted glass with a pattern on and drop them in and have a snow effect on it or a fire effect on it.

And what we used to do on a Sunday night: if we were packed out on the first house, there were a lot of side exit doors at the Metropole and we had a slide with an arrow on it that said, "Would the audience please be good enough to use the side exit doors". Instead of sticking a plain slide on, we used to mask it off to fit the screen and we put in this pattern with a slide on top and it looked quite effective. We had quite a lot of other slides for advertising films coming on in the near future.

We had a lot of black and white films in those days and you'd leave the footlights on right through the titles and, as soon as the last titles came on, you'd fade out the footlights. Obviously, when colour came along, as soon as you came on the censor you'd fade out the footlights - you should never have any colour footlights on a Technicolor picture.

So you were there during the War, during the air raids?

Talking about the air raids, we used to stop the film and the manager used to come on the stage and he'd say, "There's an air raid taking place. Anybody who wishes to leave may do so but the show's going to continue." After that went on for some time we just superimposed a slide on the film. When the cinema closed at night, we took it in turns fire watching. We used to get a few shillings for it. They had a beautiful foyer upstairs at the Metropole, settees and things, and we used to sleep there at night.

The Metropole must have had the most sophisticated projection room you ever worked in. What would you say was the least sophisticated?

I would say the Imperial Clapham Junction. It was a dump, the Imperial, but I loved it there. You had tears in the seats and usually you had a button to work the tabs [curtains] but at the Imperial you went down under the screen and when the picture came on you'd wind the handle. Then, when you were coming towards the end of the film, five minutes before the end, they'd say, "Who's going down to do the tabs?"

Albert Critoph in the projection room of the Imperial Clapham Junction

The Imperial Clapham Junction circa 1952. Now demolished, it later became the Ruby

Denis Norden

Denis Norden, born in 1922, is the well-known radio and television personality. His reminiscences also appear in Being There and Film Talk.

Can I ask you about people who became cinema managers? Did they go through the ranks in cinemas doing fairly menial tasks?

Yes, yes. All the ones I knew. There was a [Hyams Brothers] circuit of about ten: there was the State Kilburn, the Trocadero Elephant and Castle, the Troxy Commercial Rd, the Regal Edmonton, the Gaumont Watford, the Trocette Tower Bridge Road, and two or three others that now escape me. Most of the other managers had come up - they had made relatively slow progress upwards through the ranks. In the main, they'd come from front of house, but some of them had served what I thought was this invaluable spell of time as a projectionist which I found was a fascinating, terribly romantic sort of job. You had carbon arcs then. You had to put the carbons in and adjust them until there was a spark between them, a lovely fizzling sound, and then a sort of jump away. And the change-over from one projector to another was done with a foot pedal. And you had to look for the little white spot at the corner of the screen and judge it so there was an element of skill. It wasn't all taken over by machinery. And you had to rewind: you started in the projection room as a rewind boy, which meant after every reel that came off you rewound it by hand and every time you kept your forefinger and thumb on the film and every time you felt a ragged bit you were supposed to stop it and fix the film, repair the film, which you sometimes did and sometimes didn't, which was why films used to break a lot in those days.

"Mac at the Troc": Quentin Maclean at the organ of the Elephant and Castle Trocadero

But you always knew when someone was at that stage of their career because they always had little grooves in their forefinger and thumb. But you really felt you were handling Rita Hayworth, John Boles and all the various other names who were going through your hands, so it was a kind of very tactile thing.

Did you feel tempted to stay in projection?

No, because I was moving towards wanting to write. I knew the Hyams brothers, who ran the cinema, made films as well, and I said could I become a film screenwriter. And they said not until you learn something about films being a cinema manager. So they got me going through the ranks as a cinema manager. I never really did make it writing films, but I had my eye on eventually doing that. Now all the major cinemas - and these were very large cinemas, they were the largest suburban, or local cinemas, in London outside the West End and a lot of them were larger than the West End cinemas - they put out their own monthly magazine, which wasn't simply a list of the films which were going to be shown and local advertisements for your tea room or dry cleaners. It had articles in it and I wrote the articles which then went round the circuit. So you really felt like an author. And then I wrote - a completely dead art - cinema organ solos. Every cinema programme on the circuit included a cinema organist. We had some of the greats, such names as Quentin Maclean, Sidney Torch, Bobby Pagan, Phil Park. These were the great cinema organists of the time, and they would do a fifteen-minute spot on this kind of giant, many coloured console - it looked like a big jelly mould - that changed colours all the time. And they came up from a hole in the ground and spun round and they would pick a subject and would do a little musical programme on it - it would now be a film short, or a little television programme. So I would write the wording on the slides and I would either do parodies of popular songs or take things like Albert Catalby, master of melody, and make it last a quarter of an hour while he was playing. And we would get from Morgan Slides in Grays Inn Road these different slides at ninepence each, and project them with a background, a moving background, made by what I thought was the absolute knife-edge of technology in those days, which was a machine through which the slides were projected on this curtain, through which you would get the impression of dogs and horses jumping over a gate by a wheel going in front of a lantern, and those kind of things. And I would design those and they would go round the circuit and each organist would play them. There's not a lot of people who would claim to have practiced that art, which was mainly parody. I and the audience would sing along and they would laugh occasionally at some of the things.

Was cinema work a good job?

In a sense, it was an artificial time because the majority of my fellow workers were marking time prior to going into the forces. Of the staff of, let's say, the Trocadero - somehow it sticks in my head that there were 122 employees there, I wouldn't go to the stake as regards verifying that number - very much the largest part of that would be made up of girls. There would be an enormous number of usherettes and ice cream girls. There would be no career path there. Women weren't expected to have career paths in those days - there wasn't a woman cinema manager.

But why I was so much in love with the job - I had two loves, one was cinema, the other was another form of popular entertainment called variety, which Americans called vaudeville. Another dead art, but entirely satisfying in that it did everything that was expected of it, everything its

Stage show and double feature at the Trocadero Elephant and Castle for the week of 15 May 1939

audience wanted it to do. But you didn't have any critics - there is very little documentation about the great days of variety. But at these cinemas we did what was called cine-variety in that four times a day there would be a stage show which lasted three-quarters of an hour to an hour, in addition to two feature films and a short and a newsreel and an organ solo. This was top class variety. We had the biggest names and we staged opera there, we staged circuses. So you could be (to use a word we would never have dreamed of using in those days) creative. You could design sets, you could design lighting. I can remember now the beautiful oyster-coloured curtains that they had which would take the light and you could do all sorts of things with those.

Now the front-of-house staff didn't have any romantic aspirations. To some extent at the Trocadero Elephant and Castle the men were more or less selected on physical attributes, because it was a very tough area in those days. You had the gangs of young - they'd be called "teenage" now - youths, the two main ones called Elephant Boys and the Elephant Heads, enormous gangs like they used to have on the racecourses, the racecourse gangs. They were very tough, very rough, very brutal. We had usherettes raped, we had staff beaten up, so because we had two entrances on the corner we had eight doormen who were great big tough fellows, all of whom eventually wound up in the guards and so on, but they were selected, they were like bouncers would be.

It must have had a special atmosphere of excitement which, say, the Gaumont in Streatham didn't have?

I don't know if it was excitement. You were kept on your

toes because it was dangerous. My memories are coloured, dominated, more by a feeling of danger than of what the Palladium would have given me. The chap I took over from there had been knifed across the face coming out of the stage door. We used to toss out any gang members who were there. They used to bunk in through the exits, and then prowl and prey on people sitting on the front rows, so there would be raids on them - we would ring up the police and they would come along and collar twenty of them and just lock an exit door and keep them in the exit tunnel and just clobber them. Then they would seek their revenge and hit our staff and I was a target in my father's dinner jacket. I was seventeen and 6ft. 3in. and I was terribly thin and looked like a pair of braces. I always remember one night I was going to leave and one of the doormen said "No, don't you go. They're waiting for you. We'll take you across to the Tube." And from then on, until I left there to go to the Gaumont Watford, I had a flying wedge of doormen who used to take me across to the Tube. In the gents, the towels were roller towels, literally on rolling pins, not for cooking but they would roll round these and they would come out, this flying wedge, holding these wooden rolling pins, and I'm in the middle of them and we'd make a rush across to the Tube and I'd go to the Northern Line.

Was there somebody specifically who stage managed?

Yes, we had two wonderful stage managers. The bookings were done by one of the Hyams brothers personally. He would make up the bill and as time went on they would send out that bill in a rather expanded form around the variety theatres of England. We had a stage manager called Jim Pitman who did things - technically, it was a very shallow stage - which were on paper impossible. So we put on a full-scale circus there, which I always remember because the week we had it we put on an MGM film and the only place we could store the animals was behind the screen and, every time the MGM lion roared, the lion from the circus answered.

How did that operate when the circus was on?

You flew the screen, this bloody great iron screen, brought down the iron curtain, closed the big house tabs. Up came the organ. He'd give you a quarter of an hour during which time you set up the circus. You ran it out through the side into a kind of big backyard we had there with caravans, and you had everything in a circus: we had liberty horses, we had elephants, we had the lot. In fact there was a man called Aubrey Flanagan, the editor of the British edition of the Motion Picture Daily, who used to come down. I got friendly, and he rang me up in a disguised voice the week before. It was when the blackout was on and I was alone on the Sunday, and the circus was on the Monday and they were due to get in at eight o'clock. I got this call to say that the elephants are coming along the Old Kent Road. Because of the blackout, they're going to tie up their link tails and the one at the end has a rear light. They weren't supposed to get in till the morning but in those days transport was crazy so you just had to be prepared. So would I be prepared with something like a dozen bales of hay. This was the Elephant and Castle, half-past eight on the Sunday night.

What about the Hyams brothers? Did they concern themselves?

They were very much behind the scenes figures, shadowy figures. There were three of them actually: there was Phil Hyams, Sid Hyams, and Mick. Mick went to the States where he was very successful running what they call art houses there. Then he got into movies, which left Phil and Sid. They launched Collins and Grade Agents with Lew Grade who became ATV. They were very much powers behind the scenes for all sorts of entertainment.

We did a spell where we ran amateur talent nights on Sundays. At times I would be in charge of this whole cinema at seventeen-and-a-half on a Sunday. And one of the Sundays I was on my own as manager, full house and the crowd very rowdy, I didn't know what to do. I really didn't. And Mr. Phil and Mr. Sid we used to call them. They used to pay visits. I looked round and there was Mr. Phil and he came into the foyer where I was gnawing my knuckles, wondering what to do with this row going on in the auditorium. He said, "What's going on here?" I said, "They're chy-iking a bit." He said, "Leave it to me." On the stage is a girl singing "Down in the woods I can hear a brown bird singing", the sort of thing which used to be howled down. And he just walked down the centre aisle, up onto the centre stage and he puts his hand up and says, "You know who I am", and there's quiet. "I'm Phil Hyams. I own this place, I built it, I book it. Everything is down to me. I'm going to tell you a story. We once ran an amateur talent night some time ago and I was round the back, round the dressing room, and I heard the sound of sobbing", he said. "And I went round and there was a singer there, a North Country girl, and she was crying her eyes out. I said, 'What's the matter?' She said, 'I can't go out there and face them. They're too much for me. I can't face them.' I said, 'Listen, this is a South London audience, Old Kent Road people. These are the roughest, toughest people in London, but I'll tell you this: they're the fairest,' I said. 'You give them a chance, they'll give you a chance, I'll promise you.' She said, 'All right, Mr. Phil' and she went out there

always taken you into my confidence. I've got a problem. The seats are lousy, literally. As you're sitting in them, you're probably getting bitten. Well, I can't afford to put new ones in unless I put the prices up. I know you can't afford the prices. So," he said, "your choice: either you sit here and get bitten or I put the prices up."

Presumably in the afternoon you did get a lot of women and it wasn't a problem to go in on your own as a woman?

"A very special place": the auditorium of the Elephant and Castle Trocadero with its 3,500 seats (1930 photograph)

and I'll tell you who that girl was. That was Gracie Fields." And they stood up and cheered, and he came back and came up to the office and I said, "That's a wonderful story." "It's a pack of lies," he said.

He had this other little cinema. It was the one they started, a tiny little place, and a kind of great gay haunt actually, at that time [the Biograph Victoria]. Apparently he did the same thing. He walked up on the stage - they didn't have variety there, just films - but at any rate he walked up, put the lights up. He said, "You know who I am. Phil Hyams. I have to tell you something. I've always worked with you, I've

I don't think they did. They went in twos. Women went about in twos in those days, and very rarely did you get the lone woman. We had behind the cashier's grille, above the grille, a kind of wanted list, photographs of the ladies who frequented the Troc and pleasured you sitting down for various prices. There was one with a greasy black fringe called Toss-Off Kate

who would go back four rows and up her prices in the way we upped our prices.

We always guaranteed so many rows at sixpence. I think there were 400 seats at sixpence, but as you went back the price got progressively higher. We would change the prices according to what we'd think we'd take. The most successful films or programme you'd obviously try to get more out of it, but you'd play fair: you always gave these sixpenny seats, and it was full from the moment we opened to the moment we closed and we did four shows a day. There was a place called Spurgeon's Tabernacle in South London, a landmark not far away, and [during the War] a land mine hit it and blew away one of the canopies on one of the entrances. We always had 400 people waiting in the queue for the sixpennies, they'd wait three hours, and we didn't lose one of the queue. So it was a very special place.

The Hyams brothers had certain rules. One of the rules was, put simply, you must never show a white screen. You know what that means? The footlights must always go up and there be a colour on it, always be magic - if you see a white screen, it immediately tells you that you are in a cinema, that it wasn't real, it was a film. To this day, I can't bear it when you go in and the curtains open in complete silence. We never let them hear the sound of the curtain. We always played what used to be called the panatrobe, the music on the p.a. [public address system]. You kept the music going so it drowned the noise of the curtains opening - it was oiled, it seemed to swish open silently.

You had to meet the patrons - we used to call them patrons, not "pay-trons", the short 'a' - in the lobby, six o'clock change into evening dress. People had the same seats every week and sometimes it would pass from father to son, the same seat in the cinema. You were expected to know them by name and greet them. A big thing because in this kind of depressed area, to be greeted by your name, you were somebody - you might have a very menial job in a factory or something like that, but when you came into the cinema it was "Hello, Mr. Brown, you'll enjoy it tonight."

You were also there at the end of the performance, and that was a time that made a very deep impression on me because you saw the difference - if you'd lived through that, you'd know the difference between films and television. People came out of the cinema and they were still living the film till they got outside the glass doors. In other words, you stood in the foyer, you knew what time was out so you'd get there two minutes before the film would end. They always played the National Anthem, but you always opened the doors at the end of the film because there was this rush to beat the National Anthem. The people would come out, and the look on their faces - they were transported, there were still the crinkles around their eyes. Now people don't do weepies, but they were very popular in those days. They loved weepy films. Not only did they take an apple and an orange and chocolate bar and those kind of things, they took handkerchiefs (there were no Kleenex tissues), some people took boxes of handkerchiefs, and we used to talk about them as a three-hanky movie, depending on how much you cry. You would see them coming out, and men, and they didn't see you at all. They walked right past you. Now these were people who you greeted on the way in, but you knew better than to greet them on the way out. You never asked them then what they thought of it. When they came the following week, you would say then, "What did you think of the film last week?" Because they were still in the dream - you didn't disturb it. And that made a very deep impression on me.

There's nothing like it for taking you into dreams.

It's community, it's that group experience. It multiplies itself if you are there with a whole cinema full of people. I remember what Paul Jennings wrote once about *The Thurber Carnival*, a review of Thurber's work. It was on in the West End. I thought it was lovely, but it wasn't very successful. He wrote that when it finished there was a moment of total silence and in that silence everybody in the theatre was one person. Without being pompous about it, we did that nightly with this crap from Hollywood, the studio system turning out Joan Crawford rubbish. We worked on them and, whatever this Greek tragedy is supposed to give you, they got it. And once you've seen that happen, it is an unforgettable thing.

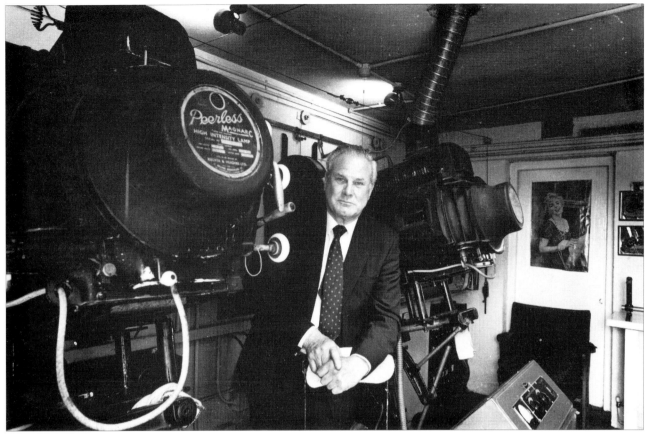

Norman Waring in his projection box at the Plaza Oxted

Norman Waring

Norman Waring, born in 1924, remains very much in the film business, running his own independent single-screen cinema, the Plaza at Oxted, Surrey.

What are your earliest memories of the cinema?

I remember going to the old Victory Cinema in Tooting Broadway, which became the Vogue. I think it was a double feature and one was a silent film. I was taken by my brother and I can remember the titles. And the other film was one of those biblical things. And then I used to go a lot to the Broadway Palace at Tooting and from there on I used to go to the old Central at Tooting Bec which became the Classic. I just used to go to the cinema an awful lot.

Was it always your brother who took you?

No. I used to disappear off on my own. But things were different then. Young boys could go out and no problems at all. I was a bit of a loner. The other cinema was the old Astoria at Tooting. They put a new front on it. It would have been mid-1930s. It was a long narrow hall, with little boxes at the side. I used to go to Balham. The Palladium right next to the station - you could hear the trains rumbling by. The Pavilion - that used to be roller skating. Very long, narrow place, very small screen.

What about the Streatham cinemas?

I used to go in the Golden Domes to see films and the other one was the Empire at Streatham Station. And there was the "Thrale", at Thrale Road, Mitcham Lane. That was a real wooden forme job, that was. I only ever went there once but my brother used to go quite often. That was an open-and-shut place. Sometimes it would be open. It ran into financial trouble. People think everything was very buoyant all the time but I don't think it was - because there was another cinema at Tooting, I think it was called the Regent, going towards Wimbledon on the left, that used to open and close, so obviously things couldn't have been all that great. Then, of course, Streatham got big new cinemas like the Astoria. I used to go to the Astoria a lot, and the Golden Domes. I remember the Astoria being built because I had an uncle who used to live up there. I remember the Granada Tooting being

The Vogue Tooting as the Cinenews in 1936

built, the big site there. It had a big traction engine, steam engines, big steam rollers there. The Granada used to hold a birthday celebration every year. There used to be an enormous cake in the foyer and you used to get a piece of this cake.

The Classic at Tooting Bec during a phase of showing foreign films

Was there variety on there, do you remember?

Yes, yes. The organ was always featured more at the Granada but there was variety. But the biggest variety, of course, was at the Astoria. That, in that area, put the most elaborate variety on. Billy Cotton used to be there a lot, Arthur Askey, all those people. In fact, they used to have an Austin Seven come on, a chap used to come through it, an act, and I remember my uncle who was in the motor business used to supply this car for them from the garage. Because they'd quite a big scene dock, you could get it on at the back. There used to be a lot of variety at the Astoria and I think that was one of the things that brought the theatre into financial trouble. The overheads were quite big there.

And a programme I always remember the Astoria used to do, maybe once a year: they'd have a different film every day which was quite unusual. All Paramount pictures, because it was controlled by Paramount then. And at the Astoria it was a seven day show. It didn't change on a Sunday, it was round for the seven days.

Did you have particular tastes when you were a boy in the Thirties?

Yes. Warner Oland/Charlie Chan, always a favourite.

Westerns, of course: Tom Mix, Buck Jones, but that was because we used to go to the Broadway Palace because it was cheap. It was fourpence as far as I remember, but it was always cheaper.

I went to the Vogue when it re-opened. Classics were looking for theatres. They opened it as a news theatre. The Spanish Civil War was on. I remember that because I was always interested in War things. They ran it for about six weeks as a news theatre and it was no good. I think they called it the CineNews.

When Classic took the old Central at Tooting Bec, they ran that. The Vogue would run the Warner Bros. and such like, and the Classic would always run the better films - the MGM films, *The Great Waltz*, this sort of stuff. It used to do very well. Always big queues at the Classic. Unbelievable. Just a feature and shorts, news. News was always three days behind, a bit cheaper.

When war started, did you continue cinema-going?

I started to work in a cinema. I started at the Gaumont Streatham. Actually I worked for The Times newspaper to start with. I got disenchanted with it. I couldn't get an apprenticeship.

How did you get the cinema job?

I used to see the Kine Weekly on the news stand and look at it, and they were advertising for projectionists - I think they were called operators in those days. And I went along to the Dominion Tottenham Court Road to see somebody and then I was told to go to Streatham. I was there with *Citizen Kane*.

It wasn't a big hit?

No. It wasn't a big hit at all.

Did it have any impact on you?

Yes. When people ask me what films stick out in my mind, I always say *Citizen Kane*, *All Quiet on the Western Front* and maybe *Paths of Glory* later.

Citizen Kane *at the Gaumont Streatham in February 1942*

The auditorium of the Gaumont Palace Streatham with projection box over the circle (1932 photograph)

What position did you have at the Gaumont?

Just a trainee projectionist.

Were you a rewind boy?

Rewind, yes, and all the general things you did in those days. It was a very large theatre, plenty of room. You had the foyer, two cash desks in the centre, aisle up left and right for the cafe, then you had an inner foyer which was the cloakrooms and cafe-restaurant, a large stage, a Compton organ (Charles Manning was on it sometimes), orchestra... You had another pay desk down the side of the cinema, on the right hand side, which was the front stalls which I think was ninepence, and you could go in the side and they had queueing facilities there and then you entered the front of the place.

Yes, a very nice theatre. Sound was very good. It was about a 2,500 seater. I've seen that full, with queues, many a time.

And the projection room itself?

Very large. Very clean. Everything was kept absolutely immaculate. There were three projectors - Gaumont Eclipse, BA sound and Hall and Connelly arcs. It had two spotlights, no slide lanterns (I don't think Gaumont-British had slide lanterns at all in any of their theatres), two large amplifiers on the back wall which as you put the key in to open they used to go off, and a fader in the centre. Quite a rake because the projection box used to overhang the circle. There were about five of us there.

What were the hours like?

Half-past ten to the end, really, which could be half-past ten at night.

How many days off a week?

One day.

Never Saturday?

No. Never Saturday. You'd get a Sunday because, I think I'm right in saying, that under the Health and Safety regulations, if you were under sixteen you couldn't work on a Sunday. But then what I used to do was go down to the Empress at Brixton and work there on a Sunday because they used to show films then.

Did you work a seven-day week because you needed the money?

No .

Because you wanted to work?

Fascination, really. The trick there was you had to be off ten o'clock on a Sunday - the LCC licensing. So you'd start at half-past three and you had two long features - it wasn't a feature and a second feature, you'd get a double Errol Flynn or a double Deanna Durbin which ran maybe three hours with the intermissions - so, on the first run or somewhere, the odd reel, well, get rid of that. Or a quick change-over was done to get it off by ten o'clock, because the licensing people were most strict on this. It used to do very well business-wise on a Sunday. Presumably flat-rate bookings. It used to be Universal films and Warner Bros. films.

What was the projection room like?

Very cold projection box. I don't think there was any heating up there. I worked there for a couple of months, I suppose. I used to wear an overcoat a lot of the time or a pullover and a coat. Terrific rake - the portholes were about the edge of the floor. Front shutter projectors and BTP sound, and again Hall and Connelly arcs. A very big mercury rectifier there - enormous thing, quite Frankensteinish.

What was the risk of nitrate fires?

All the projectors had the fire traps. The big problem was with people opening the top spool box, the fire going up into it. There was no smoking whatsoever in the box. Always two in the projection room, that was the licensing regulations.

Did you have a procedure for checking the reels were in the right order?

Oh yes. With G.-B. in particular, you had a sheet and you signed who laced it up, who rewound it, what time it went on, and the time the complete programme ended. Every reel, if you laced it, you signed it, and the person on the other machine would come round and check it, sign it, and then who rewound it, and you'd sign it, and who showed it, of course.

An odd thing with G.-B.: on the change-overs, you know you've got the dots - they'd paint white just about where the dot was. The only place I've ever seen this. Whether it was, because of the throws of some of these places, you might miss the dot whereas if you're looking at the projector you can see the white paint go through... And different cinemas used to use different colours. Some would have white for a motor and red for an over, and some the other way round, and some would use all blue, and you'd get quite a combination of these different coloured water paints.

Where did you go after the Gaumont?

I went over to the Regal. I got itchy feet, I'm afraid. I was always fascinated by other places. I was trying to get experience - this was the thing. I was still at the bottom, but a bit more money, I suppose, because originally the Gaumont was twelve shillings and sixpence.

That was, relatively, quite good pay.

I don't know - it was a 66-hour week you used to work. It wasn't good but it could have been a lot worse.

Did you feel deprived about having to work every night?

Yes, in some ways. Obviously there was not much of a social life. That's why one would talk to usherettes.

When you went to the Regal and worked for another major circuit [ABC], was there any real difference?

It was very efficient but not quite so grand as the Gaumont. Projection box was nice - it had a parquet floor and tiles. Working conditions were good. But the theatre for the show was the Astoria though I still think the Gaumont was the better theatre.

The Golden Domes Streatham, still closed in April 1948

Was the Golden Domes still open?

The week the Regal opened, the Golden Domes shut. ABC still kept it. Classics were very interested in taking it because Classics were expanding and it would have been an ideal Classic repertory cinema because they were very successful. But it was opposition to ABC, so nothing ever came of it.

We used to go down to the Golden Domes to check it over, that the building was safe. All the equipment was still in there, everything was there as they shut it. They'd say, go down and get some oil or something. It was kept shut right through the War. I think the Post Office used the back of it for something.

Did you have special precautions during the War for evacuation and so on?

The Regal used to put a slide on saying that there was an air-raid on and you could either leave or stay .

You didn't get your money back if you went?

No, no. A lot of people stayed. You always had a stand-by programme, not because of the War or anything like that, but for let-downs. If there was a heavy air-raid, in some cases you would run on after the closing time and you could use this programme for that. The other thing at the Regal you used to do was called fire-watching. Incendiary bombs was the main thing: if an incendiary bomb came down, you could put it out. You used to stay there all night.

What happened with the glass in the chandeliers?

A lot of glass was taken out and stored. And in a lot of cases blue lamps were put in. Lighting was reduced in the foyers. Nothing on outside: no neon or the name of the cinema. The Regal, you had that great thing which you used to climb up on a ladder and stick all the lettering and it would all light up behind. All that sort of thing was switched off. Also, there was a drive to save electricity anyway and you weren't supposed to use a lot of house lighting.

What about refreshments during the War?

There was ice-cream and the restaurant at the Gaumont was open as well, which you did with coupons.

Did you rehearse any of the programmes?

On a Monday, which was the first day at Streatham, there used to be a big cue sheet with the various fader settings. And you'd have a fader in the circle: it was the end seat, front seat on the right of the back part of the circle. It was a remote control one. The chief used to sit there and you could press it up and press it down. You ought to have been able to switch the thing off but it was permanently wired in and if somebody sat there and they leaned against this thing, the sound used to go right up. It happened a number of times.

Did you ever work at the Astoria?

Yes, I worked there when I came out of the army as second projectionist.

How did the Astoria compare with the Regal and the Gaumont?

It was a bit run-down, I thought, generally. It had been run by Odeon then for quite a while. A lot of the equipment had been taken out of the box. There were only two machines up there where there used to be four.

Still the cafe?

No, that had gone. The soda fountain had gone. I think Odeon were a more cheese-paring company. They were always very penny-pinching. I didn't last there, couldn't stand it. I got fed up working evenings and weekends, especially as I'd had a break from it in the Army.

You were in a world of your own in the projection box.

Yes. You were controlling it all - more so then than now with all the technology. I think it was more magic. In those days where you had more than one projector - two projectors, three projectors - and spotlights and a Brenograph, and if you had to wear white coats and smocks, if you took people up to a projection box they were absolutely fascinated.

The Telekinema that became the first NFT

Leslie Hardcastle

Leslie Hardcastle, born in 1926, is Curator of the Museum of the Moving Image, following his many years in charge of the National Film Theatre. He is also featured in Being There.

My uncle was a film actor and I used to go to all the studios and meet all the directors and Paul Robeson, Phyllis Calvert and James Mason and all these people when I was a kid. It was very intoxicating. I would like to have gone into film production but I ended up in the film distribution department of a film company. I was a nurse in the Navy for two and a half years. Around that time I also worked for British Lion Films as a production assistant at Borehamwood and then I went to their head office where I was in "bars" and "cross-overs" and the commercial side of the film industry. And, this particular section of the company, we used to book for prisons, borstals, film societies, universities and cultural organisations. And one day somebody suggested that I'd be happier in an organisation that was actually concerned with those things rather than the commercial side of the film industry. And I went along to the British Film Institute and got a job running the Central Booking Agency which booked films for the then very expanded film society movement in this country. Because I came from Wardour Street, I knew all the renting companies and I could speak their language because I'd learned it while I was there - bad language and trade language - and I was able to negotiate these films for the film society movement.

What was the BFI like in those days?

It was very small then, but it was a pioneering organisation. Staff used to come rushing in saying, "We've found the missing reel of Rex Ingram's *Four Horsemen of the Apocalypse!*" We were so pleased with such discoveries we would all go out for a drink to celebrate.

The National Film Archive collected films but we had nowhere to show them. The British Film Institute started in 1933 but it wasn't until 1951, when the Festival of Britain came, that the BFI acquired a cinema.

The British Film Institute was asked to run the cinema side of the Festival. The Festival buildings were all architectural and engineering feats, each containing a tribute to British achievements in law, shipbuilding, science, and so on. Fortunately enough for us, cinema was of so little interest to the planners so they located the Telekinema in a remote part of the Festival site. That became very useful later on, for no one was immediately interested in developing the part of the site that had housed the Telekinema.

And you could actually see the projection as well.

Yes, the projection box had a rear wall of glass. The public could see the projectionists working. It was a remarkable cinema. So were its programmes.

Is that where you got the idea for MOMI?

Yes. The MOMI cinema also has a projection box with a

rear glass window just like the Telekinema. In the Telekinema, the projection box used to form part of the foyer. The shape of the cinema was also quite revolutionary - the circle had a university-lecture theatre raked floor and the stalls sloped upwards towards the floating screen. But that was before CinemaScope. It wouldn't have worked for CinemaScope. Remember, the Telekinema could only show movies at standard size ratio.

The projection box of the Telekinema with its transparent rear wall

What was the building like? Did it look like a hut?

No. It was a very modern building. There was only one thing wrong with it. It was built of temporary building materials which would only last six months - the length of the Festival. We occupied it in the hope we could stay there for five years. Shell were then going to construct their building over the site. People really don't realise that the Telekinema, later NFT, was originally kept up simply because it was dearer to pull it down. We had discovered that it was going to cost £7,000 to demolish the building and clear the site. We asked Shell: "If we pay for it to be pulled down, will you let us keep it up for five years?" And they said yes. The government, who gave a small grant to the British Film Institute, said, "No, we don't want you to do this." It was left to the LCC who owned the only permanent building of the Festival of Britain to say okay and allow us to keep the building up and to rename it the National Film Theatre.

People you ask about the Festival of Britain seem to particularly remember the Telekinema.

Yes, it was an interesting place. If you remember, it was only six years after the War. It was absolutely remarkable that in the Telekinema you could see large screen television, stereophonic sound and three dimensional films which were really something in those days.

The LCC were very impressed by the Telekinema's great success. Nearly a quarter of a million people went through the Telekinema in the Festival. Also, during the Festival I think people walked around and got terribly tired. They were glad to sit down by going to the pictures. The show was an hour long. We could get four hundred people in and out in just six minutes. Change a house in six minutes.

And did you have a lot to do with the Telekinema?

Yes. I located all the films that were shown for the six years Karel Reisz was the programmer. The first film we showed on 20th October 1952 was *Neighbours* by Norman McLaren and the second film was *Pygmalion*. I was very young in those days and low down in the pecking order of the Institute.

Every film we showed in those days was a great discovery. What people don't realise is that today you can see the whole world of cinema either at the National Film Theatre or on television. The National Film Theatre alone shows 2,000 films a year. You can now buy videos of the film classics. In those days films were just not available. They weren't in the country to start with. The number of specialised cinemas were also limited: you had Studio One and Two in Oxford Street, the Academy, the Curzon and the Everyman Hampstead, and that was it. They screened mainly French films. You also had the Film Society movement which worked on both 35mm and 16mm.

It was my job to find films, negotiate films or import films. I sometimes had to persuade film renters to keep films in the country and not destroy them. Some renters knew nothing about these now classic films. Others absolutely hated foreign films because they didn't make them money. Frequently they had been stuck with these films as part of another deal. We had to make them available for the NFT and the Film Society

movement. It took about six to seven pioneering years to get only a few prints available.

It is also not generally known that, when the National Film Theatre was started, the government didn't want BFI grant money to go into it and ruled that it had to be completely self-supporting, and indeed it was for twenty-six years.

And there were many other difficulties. Film supply, for instance. The film trade who owned the films said, "We'll allow the NFT to open but only on a membership basis." This is why we had membership. They insisted that films be shown in seasons rather than just show individual films. They ruled, after you become a member, you must wait forty-eight hours before you were admitted, and that we mustn't advertise the titles in the papers. At one stage, the Cinema Exhibitors Association, London Branch, ruled that we had to submit all our programmes for scrutiny before we were allowed to book them. I spent my whole time trying to outwit these people.

Later on, the commercial people began to realise there was money to be made from these films. In the Fifties and Sixties, Classic Cinemas were a very good group of cinemas. They started showing these films and they didn't like the NFT showing them first.

Was NFT programming considered to be controversial?

People in government and licensing were sensitive about the political nature of the films. Soon the whole process of showing certain films became a little tricky. The BFI were a government supported organisation and questions were sometimes asked of the Board of Governors and sometimes in the House. We were challenged, "Why did we show this film?" "Why did we show that film?"

Ken Wlaschin, of all NFT Programme Officers, pushed the realms of censorship, of acceptance of political comment, of social acceptance of certain types of movies, more than any other person. We were pioneers at the NFT.

It could also have its funny side. In one week I had letters of protest saying I was a homosexual, I was a fascist, I was a communist, just because of the nature of the films we had shown in one week. Sometimes they challenged our right to show certain films.

We, however, felt it imperative that they should be shown

and went ahead. The only time the National Film Theatre did get leant on concerned an event, not a film. Frank Hazell, my predecessor, did the most difficult thing you could possibly do in the late Fifties - he booked Leni Riefenstahl for a lecture. Suddenly the iceman didn't cometh in the bar, the bread it didn't arrive from the Jewish baker, Paramount rang up and cancelled the Gary Cooper programme, the Czech Embassy threatened to cancel their National Film Week if Leni Riefenstahl came to the country...

The National Film Theatre

When was that?

'56, '58 - somewhere around there. We were in constant trouble. Once we arranged a week of Israeli films just when terrorists were blowing them up. Sometimes even a little season could prove to be explosive. The Montenegran season got us into real trouble. You wouldn't imagine that a four-day Montenegran season would result in a riot outside the NFT, but it did. The house manager was hit on the head by protesting women during a season on women's rights. The NFT was a centre of controversy in those days.

Also, in the Fifties and Sixties, people felt very strongly about political issues. I don't think you could feel as strongly today about those subjects. In the Sixties, Godard came to the NFT to a public discussion over the right of his producer to change his film's ending. Students staged an alternative show outside using Godard's second copy, which he preferred. Suddenly their dynamo broke down - I gave them electricity to keep them outside as there was also the possibility that the students were about to stage a sit-in in NFT 1. Suddenly, Godard hit the producer on the nose on stage and Mr. Wesson, who was our manager at that time, carried off Mr. Godard while people from Black Power hit him and tried to prevent Wesson from doing so. Godard called out, "Go and get your money back and give it to Black Power" - which fifty people did. I then sold those tickets to another fifty people who had been queuing to get into the cinema.

The NFT was a very exciting place, an enormously exciting place. But it had hundreds of problems. Now, of course, the whole atmosphere's entirely different. Renters actually come to you before they release their films. They like a celebrity lecture involving the director and leading actor and a preview at the NFT before it starts its West End run.

What about the John Player lectures in the late Sixties?

Unbelievably successful. Having negotiated the series, the first mistake I made was to link four speakers - Jacques Tati, Jean-Luc Godard, Carl Foreman and Truffaut - with supporting seasons of their work all in the same booklet. This was the inaugural lecture of the series. All the John Player Board of Directors and all the Board of the Governors of the British Film Institute were to be there. Jacques Ledoux, the director of the Cinémathèque Belgique, came to town to see me and said, "I see you have Godard on Sunday to give a lecture. You know that Godard is going through an emotive period and we've just been disappointed by him. I don't think he's going to come to London."

I leapt on a plane to Paris, taking with me a young lady who could speak French. I discovered I could communicate better on my own than with the help of the interpreter. I had discovered a taxi driver who used to appear in Godard films. Together we chased Godard around Paris. I finally found him at the Cinémathèque and I gave him his air ticket. Godard said, "I'll try to come", and then rushed out after trying to escape from the room through a cupboard.

He didn't come. He sent a telegram instead, saying, "Give my fee to the first person you see on the street for it's the man in the street who's creating the cinema future." This proved to be quite embarrassing, because we had not intended to pay speaker's fees. The whole event was a disaster. I then rushed off to Paris a second time to see the next speaker, Jacques Tati, and explained the honour of France was at stake and that he must come to London. Tati was wonderful. He actually came three times to the NFT. The only trouble was that he was the most serious man I've ever met in my life and the two weekends I spent with Jacques Tati nearly gave me a nervous breakdown. He just worried about everything. He worried about politics, about his work, about money. But he was unbelievably funny - once he was on stage, the audience wouldn't let him off.

Were these lectures all over-subscribed?

Oh yes, always. Many of the lectures were televised, which meant we were always concerned over the timing of the guest's arrival. We had arranged for Graham Greene to be televised and thought he had let us down. It was just five minutes before starting time and suddenly a car stopped outside the NFT, out got Graham Greene, and he gave a terrific interview. Five minutes after his lecture we turned around and he was no longer there. Just like one of his films.

Bette Davis was quite remarkable. She was interviewed by Joan Bakewell, who was the arts correspondent for the BBC at that time, and I thought it was very good that she chose this lovely girl to interview her even though she upstaged her all the way through in the nicest of ways.

When I collected Bette Davis from the hotel, she asked me did I know who the lighting cameraman was. I said I could find out. She asked to see him on arrival. I explained that we had the BFI Board of Governors and John Player's directors. Davis said, "If you don't mind, I'd like to see the lighting cameraman first." When she met him, she said, "My name is Bette Davis. I like a haze on a 4 and a monkey on a 2..." She just knew that the most important person there for Bette Davis was this professional. It was strange to observe a great

star like Bette Davis was nervous before going on stage, but then a true professional always is. They never disregard their audience. Every audience is a challenge and cannot be taken for granted.

Has the South Bank gone through a lot of changes?

There was a period, about the late Sixties-Seventies, when we just went through hell for about six years because of reconstruction work on the South Bank. They were realigning Waterloo Bridge immediately behind us, realigning the river bank right in front of us. Bang bang bang went the steam hammer. They were building the Hayward Gallery and the Queen Elizabeth Hall on one side of us and the Royal National Theatre on the other side. We were walled up three times. You could arrive in the morning and discover that you couldn't get into the building because the builders' hoardings had been moved over night. We were set on fire twice, £78,000 worth of damage was done by lorries bumping into us.

But our membership hung on. Despite all the disruption and building work, they actually still attended. There was one poor lady - I can tell you what she was wearing: a leopard skin coat and matching crocodile shoes and handbag - and she was the wife of a Harley Street specialist - she actually fell into a 6ft. pool of wet cement. Fortunately it wasn't our cement - it was the LCC's. Everyone laughs about this poor lady now. She was brought into the foyer in a very grave state. The head usherette was short-sighted and, it being the time of the Swinging Sixties, people wore all sorts and styles of make-up and she thought: funny grey make-up all over. She put her glasses on and realised...

What sort of audiences did you get in the Sixties?

I think we had lots of different audiences. They tended to change with the movies. People then were interested in one particular form of cinema: a subject or a language. Once we had an Egyptian programme and it was absolutely packed to suffocation because you suddenly realised there was a large population of Egyptians living and working in London at that time and they were coming to hear their native tongue. We do not get as many Poles now, they're a very close society, and they also used to come to hear their native tongue.

The first Communist Chinese season ever staged in Europe was held at the NFT before China was admitted to the United Nations, and it resulted in all BFI staff sticking 27,000 bits of paper over Norman McLaren's films in our booklet. We'd foolishly put the McLaren films in as the support for the opening of the Chinese Season because McLaren had gone to China to advise on the setting up of an animation school in Shanghai. The Chinese appeared to have thoroughly checked the records and found out that his airfare had been paid for by an agency which was part of an agency serving UNESCO, and UNESCO was part of the UNO and they weren't in the UNO and consequently they weren't going to give us the films. I finally managed to persuade the Chinese Embassy to release all the films providing we removed the Norman McLaren film from the booklet. We had 27,000 members at the time. We literally had to get all the Institute staff to come together and stick 27,000 bits of paper over 27,000 Norman McLarens in 27,000 booklets.

The only thing I hadn't thought of happened: I'd got the films, I had an invited audience, all was set, but the chief operator, a wonderful man called Charles Beddow, came to see me and said, "What do I do now? I can't speak Chinese." The films had been delivered but all the labels were in Chinese. Fortunately, we found a student from King's College right across the road who could speak Mandarin. That's how we got the movies onto the screen.

It was all one adventure after another. Disaster became our middle name. Now everything goes more or less to routine. People never notice the snags. It was much more fun in those days.

Ellen Bailey outside the former Granada Clapham Junction

Ellen and David Bailey

Ellen and David Bailey, born in 1928 and 1927 respectively, met and married while working at the Granada Clapham Junction. Today they live nearby, at Balham.

EB: I was born in Lowestoft in Suffolk. I remember going to the Saturday morning pictures but you couldn't usually hear anything, there was so much noise. And I always remember going to the Odeon to see *The Adventures of Tom Sawyer*. I cried my eyes out. Apart from that, I can't remember much about my childhood.

Did your parents take you to the cinema?

EB: Well, we had a shop at the time and it was rather difficult for them. I had three elder brothers and I either went with them or friends.

When did you move to London?

EB: At the start of the War. My father was in the navy and he was stationed at Chatham and we had relatives in Earlsfield [Southwest London] so we all moved up here. We weren't in London long when my father was moved to the Isle of Man, so we went over there for fifteen months. Then I came back to London when I was fourteen. I had a job over in Streatham for one year. And then one of the ladies in the office said to me, "Would you like to change your job?" I said, "I don't know." So she said, "Well, it's at the Granada Clapham Junction", and she named a figure - I think it was thirty-five shillings a week - and she said, "You don't have to

The auditorium of the Granada Clapham Junction in 1937

start until ten o'clock." This lady spoke for me and I went. It was another ten shillings on my wages and I took the job.

I was there right until I left to have our first child, which was eight years. And I was actually chief cashier by the time I was eighteen. I remember the prices: they were ninepence, one shilling, one shilling-and-threepence, one shilling-and-ninepence, two shillings-and-threepence, and three shillings-and-sixpence. I think the ninepence was probably for children. The one shillings were right down the front. Then one shilling-and-ninepence and two shillings-and-threepence. And then two shillings-and- ninepence and three shillings-and-sixpence were upstairs.

Did you like working there?

EB: Oh, I loved it. It was always busy and I didn't even mind working weekends. I just took it in my stride that it was a job and if I wanted to stay in the job I'd got to work weekends. Then after a few years I went up to the office where they used to buy all the chocolates and sweets for the whole circuit. And the uniform department was up there as

well. Anyone wanted a uniform, they would send them to Clapham Junction to be measured up.

Chocolates and sweets stopped during the War?

DB: They still gave the ration tickets. You were involved in taking their ration tickets as well as their money. Anybody buying, you had to take that coupon. There was a particular Mars bar representative that took a shine to Ellen and used to feed her broken Mars bars.

When did you join the Granada?

DB: I'd come out of the services. I'd gone into the services at eighteen and I did eighteen months. I was discharged medically unfit. I went into the cinema just after that, so I'd be just about twenty.

The Granada Clapham Junction in 1937

And where were you brought up?

DB: I lived in Battersea in my youth but I suffered a lot of illness, rheumatic fever and things like that.

When you were little, did you go to the cinema?

DB: Yes. I used to go to Saturday morning cinemas and

Ellen Bailey on the roof of the Granada with staff members, Mr. Grimshaw (in uniform), Mr. Hurst and Mr. Waddington

used to go to the Super Palace. Always something going on there. That was in York Road, Battersea. That was where you got sing-alongs and all that sort of thing. It was right in the heart of Battersea and you got all the real old Londoners in there for a good sing-along and then the films. They had a fantastic organ there which was all colours of the rainbow, all lights.

And we used to go to the Savoy in York Road when I was a youngster. And we lived next door to a pet shop and he used to display a board outside for a cinema: he was an elderly man and he used to give my mother the free tickets to go, and that was the Pavilion Lavender Hill.

So you got romantically attached at the Granada?

EB: That was when we first met.

DB: When I was standing on the door, doing the relief doorman. The fluttering of eyelashes from the cashbox...

What was your uniform?

DB: I didn't put a uniform on. I just used to put a smock on while I was relief for half an hour. I didn't have a full uniform.

Do you remember the doorman's uniform?

DB: Yes. It was blue, gold buttons, and gold braid.

And you had to handle queues...

DB: There used to be queues. If the weather got bad, we used to have a crush hall where we put them in, rather than have long queues outside. And then they'd call from the cash box "Room for ten" and filter ten through. The two cash boxes were either side of the foyer.

EB: Sundays particularly, I think the two cash boxes were always open.

When did you finish work in the cash box?

EB: About nine o'clock we'd have to cash up and then we'd take them upstairs with the books.

This was after the main film had started.

EB: Yes. You couldn't shut down before that.

Did many people come in at the last minute and miss the supporting film?

EB: There used to be Plough Road School. A lot of people used to go to night school there, and sometimes they used to finish their night school and pop over at the last minute to go in and see a film.

Would you say the cheapest seats always sold out first?

EB: It all depended. I think in the evening, if there was a boy taking a girl out, he would splash out a bit more, go to the back stalls.

DB: And the back of the circle.

When you were working at the Granada, did you see the films that were showing?

DB: I think one of the best series I liked when we were

both working there was the Anna Neagle/Michael Wilding series, *Spring in Park Lane* or *Maytime in Mayfair*.

What about Saturday morning pictures? How much was that?

EB: Sixpence, I think. And we used to have a card. You had to stamp a Donald Duck on the card every time the Granadiers came in. There were all squares on the card.

If they filled up the card, what happened?

EB: They'd keep the card. I'd know if they had this card they were enrolled and we used to send them a birthday card.

Were the children well behaved?

Saturday morning, after the matinee, they'd be cleaning up forever. Orange peel, apple cores, all coming down from the top onto those at the bottom. There were little hooligans in those days.

Did you talk to the patrons at all?

EB: I think you'd talk to them if you saw them regularly, like I said to one woman, "This is the fourth time you've been this week. What's the attraction?" She said, "Stewart Granger's chest does something to me." I can't remember the film. One with Margaret Lockwood, where he's swashbuckling. His shirt's all open and out comes the rapier or sword.

Stewart Granger's chest

Joan Howard outside the former Majestic/Gaumont Clapham, now a nightclub

Joan Howard

Joan Howard, born in 1928, is one of ten children brought up in Clapham. She worked as a projectionist at the local Majestic and as an usherette at the Waterloo Station News Theatre. She now lives and works in Croydon.

We used to go to Saturday morning shows because my mother had ten children, so she used to send us off out of the way. It was great. All the children used to sing just before the picture started and, of course, you always had a serial which went on and so you really had to go each week to keep up. I even remember that one of my favourite serials was *The Yellow Phantom*. I can't remember who was in it but I know he was in a room and the walls were closing in on him... You get to there, and then you have to go next week - but I couldn't go the next week.

It was good fun for the kids. It was nice because it gave the parents a morning off - send all the children off. There used to be queues miles long of kids, hundreds of them, because the Majestic [Clapham] was quite a big cinema, they could get quite a lot of children in.

Did the cinema manager come on the stage?

Yes, the manager used to come and start the kids off with a sing-song like "We come along on Saturday morning" and "greeting everybody with a smile". And the head usher there -

The Majestic circa 1946

was about fifteen or sixteen at the time. I didn't win, I might add. Richard Attenborough was one of the judges - I can't remember who else.

There were only about ten of us and you just went up on stage - nothing like it is these days. You didn't wear a bathing suit or anything like that - I wore my sister's dress, just a white top and red skirt. And I think what I did wrong was, they said: "Do you have a boyfriend?" and I said: "About eight", and I should have been demure and said I just have one. Richard Attenborough did give me a lift home. That's all he gave me - a lift home.

We've heard of kids who used to get into the Majestic without paying.

We used to bunk in. What we used to do was, one would pay and then they would go down to the exit that was near the screen. It was at the back of where the alley was, at the back of the Majestic, and you used to go and open that and about six of us would come in. We all sat in the front row right down like this so that nobody could see. We did get caught quite a lot of time.

We used to bunk in when we were older as well, when we were in our teens. You couldn't afford to go - it was one shilling and sixpence then, so one of you would pay and go and open the door. The worst part was when there's four of you comes in and there's no seats empty - the cinema was full.

How did you get into projection?

It was just advertised at the Majestic and I thought I'd like to try it. My first job was when I was thirteen and a half, in Webster's shoe shop in Brixton. I got £1 a week. I didn't like that very much and I had various other jobs. In those days it was easier to get out of one job and go into another. Then I just saw the job advertised at the Majestic one evening and I applied, got the job, and had to go for three weeks training at Holborn. It was mostly young men there - there was one other girl and myself. And on the two exam days she didn't turn up and the men helped me get through it and I passed. And I was third operator. Then, on the last couple of months I was there, I was second operator.

his name was Charlie - he had a withered arm. He was always so nice to us and always bought us sweets and he was there for donkey's years.

Did your parents take you to the cinema in the evening or the afternoon?

No. In those days when you had ten children you were very, very poor. We really were poor. So we really didn't go to the cinema during the week. It was only the Saturday shows we used to go to. I mean, we just played out in the street and things like that.

And as I grew up I even went in for a beauty competition at the Majestic. It was my mother that sent the picture in - I didn't know anything about it. In those days you sent up a picture to the Majestic and then they wrote to you. I think I

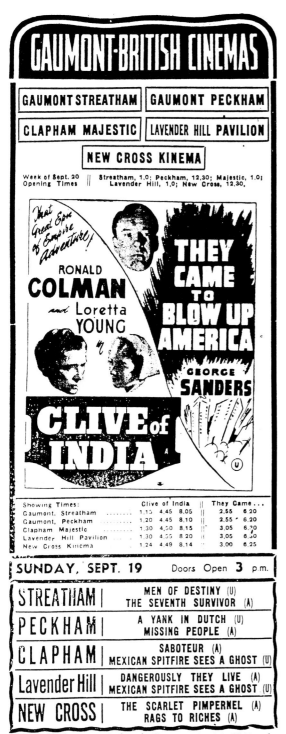

GAUMONT·BRITISH CINEMAS

GAUMONT STREATHAM	GAUMONT PECKHAM
CLAPHAM MAJESTIC	LAVENDER HILL PAVILION
NEW CROSS KINEMA	

Week of Sept. 20 Opening Times || Streatham, 1.0; Peckham, 12.30; Majestic, 1.0; Lavender Hill, 1.0; New Cross, 12.30.

That Great Epic of Empire Adventure!

RONALD COLMAN and Loretta YOUNG in

THEY CAME TO BLOW UP AMERICA

GEORGE SANDERS

CLIVE of INDIA

Showing Times:	Clive of India		They Came...
Gaumont, Streatham	1.15 4.45 8.05	||	2.55 6.20
Gaumont, Peckham	1.20 4.45 8.10	||	2.55 6.20
Clapham Majestic	1.30 4.50 8.15	||	3.05 6.20
Lavender Hill Pavilion	1.30 4.55 8.20	||	3.05 6.30
New Cross Kinema	1.24 4.49 8.14	||	3.00 6.25

SUNDAY, SEPT. 19   Doors Open 3 p.m.

STREATHAM	MEN OF DESTINY (U) THE SEVENTH SURVIVOR (A)
PECKHAM	A YANK IN DUTCH (U) MISSING PEOPLE (A)
CLAPHAM	SABOTEUR (A) MEXICAN SPITFIRE SEES A GHOST (U)
Lavender Hill	DANGEROUSLY THEY LIVE (A) MEXICAN SPITFIRE SEES A GHOST (U)
NEW CROSS	THE SCARLET PIMPERNEL (A) RAGS TO RICHES (A)

Clive of India was revived on the Gaumont circuit in 1943 and played the Majestic for the week of 20th September

What did you do as third operator?

Well, I can remember they used to have two machines in those days with the big arcs, the negative and positive, and you used to have twelve reels to a film and you'd thread them up and you'd wait, I think, twenty minutes. You'd watch and the dot would come where you would switch over to your next machine and then you'd take the reel off and rewind it. And, as you re-wound them, you had to feel for any breaks in the film which then you would cut and scrape and glue and repair. In those days you had the film for the week and then on the Saturday you'd go through all the films, make sure they weren't torn, put them into their tins ready to go to the next cinema. Then you'd have a separate film for Sunday, just for the one day.

I think the most difficult part was doing the arc. If they started going out, if you're looking at your film and it's going a bit dark, you'd look through the arc and see that the positive is wearing out and you'd have to put a new one in. That was a little more difficult than just lacing up and running a film but really and truthfully, when I think about it now, it was quite easy.

How many people worked in the projection box in all?

Three. First, second, and one who would re-wind films and that, and make cups of tea.

Do you particularly remember any of the films you showed?

I can remember the policemen used to come in if it was raining and stand inside at the back of the cinema and watch the film. The film which was on one week was *Clive of India* and there is a part where all the men are on elephants fighting and it was on the Saturday night and the policeman went over to the manager and said, "I haven't seen the fighting scene and the film's nearly over." And what we'd done, we'd missed out one of the reels but it must have been such a good switch over from one machine to the other that nobody noticed. Obviously if they hadn't seen the film they didn't know that there should have been a fighting scene in it, but we knew and there was nothing we could do about it. It was just nice because we got finished twenty minutes early. That's the one film which really sticks in my memory because this thing happened. I always remember seeing Max Miller at the Majestic. I wasn't working there then. They used to have a stage show now and then. I remember I went with my mum. They had to pull the safety curtain down on him because he was telling a rude joke. It was nothing like the jokes are today.

Did you find it a problem to have to work in the evenings?

In those days there wasn't so much going on as there is for the teenagers in these days with all the discos. There were the dance halls but one couldn't afford always to go to those places, so it wasn't too bad. If it had been today, I probably might not have done it. Six nights a week is quite a lot, and it's not as though you can pop out when you want to. And the cinemas used to finish about half-past ten, eleven o'clock, and by the time you got everything put away it used to be quite late.

The day you got off varied?

Yes. I used to have a Tuesday all day and then the following Wednesday until the evening, so it was one and a half days.

The Majestic had a sliding roof that used to open...

That's right. A very big dome. It used to open up and you see the sky and all the stars, and it was absolutely lovely. I think they used to open it up in the nice weather, in the evening, and you could look up and see the stars. And when it was closed, it was orange-looking, like an orange lit-up sky.

Was one of your jobs to open this?

No. That was nothing to do with us. We were in the operating box purely to show the films and then anything to do with the film part, that was all. Nothing to do with the

rest of the cinema at all. That was to do with the manager of the cinema. It was like he wasn't anything to do with us. He couldn't tell me what to do. My chief operator was the one who I had to answer to. If I wanted a day off, it was to do with the chief operator. And if I had any complaints, it was to do with the chief operator.

You had to put records on during the interval, presumably?

We used to have music while the slides were on - we used to have a lot of slides for putting on, for advertising. Unless the organist was playing while the slides were on. They had an organist at the Majestic who used to come up out of the bowels of the earth.

When you projected Saturday morning pictures, were the kids just as noisy?

Yes. We used to go downstairs to the kiosk sometimes to get some sweets and it used to be all the children there, a hell of a noise - but very quiet when Buck Jones was on, cowboys.

When did you go into usheretting?

I did that when I was about twenty-one, at Waterloo Station. My mother and another sister of mine worked in the News Theatre there. She got me a job there as an usherette. I think my mum must have worked round in every cinema as an usherette. I used to go and wait for my mum sometimes when she worked at the [Clapham] Pavilion as an usherette. That was a little, tiny place and when you went in you could see the women - they would look around, see if there was a fellow sitting on his own, and then go and sit next to him. I think my mum liked being an usherette purely to see the films.

Did the News Theatre's manager give you training or advice?

No, he gave you a torch and a uniform and that was it. The uniform was royal blue with gold and I think we used to have a little hat, a sort of a pill-boxy type hat. And one of us would tear the tickets and the other usherette would take them down and show them where to sit. And, of course, you had to remember how many seats you had. And some of them wanted to sit at the back and some of them wanted to sit at the front and the side and you had to go and see where you could seat them. And then, when the interval came, you would take turns each in putting the tray round you with your ice creams.

What kind of audience did you have?

Different types of people. Some had to wait for a train, they'd missed a train, they'd just go in. You got a lot of people who had come out of their offices with one of their staff and they wanted somewhere where it's dark, so what better than a news theatre? It's not going to cost you so much and you're right on top of your train so you can go home to your wife or husband. So you can pop into the News Theatre and sit there and have a little kiss and cuddle and what have you and it hasn't cost you very much, has it? If you go to a hotel, it costs you a lot more. We used to laugh about it really. My mother would come back and say, "Go and have a look at C row." And you can't see the girl, she's down on the floor. Terrible, the things that used to go on.

You never interfered?

No, you couldn't. If we came down with a torch to look for a seat, they'd pull themselves together. But we did find girls' panties and men's shorts and all sorts of things. And condoms, as we now call them - in those days they were called French letters. You used to find loads of those down in the cinema. I'd hate to have been the cleaner. But we used to go round to look because so many people left things behind, anyway - cases and handbags and things like that.

Charles Beddow in the MOMI Cinema projection room

Charles Beddow

Charles Beddow, born in 1929, has spent his entire career in and around projection boxes. He has just retired from being Technical Manager of the National Film Theatre and the Museum of the Moving Image.

I was born in Chelsea but actually I spent my childhood in Southend. I won a scholarship to the Municipal College, Southend, but it was evacuated during the War to Mansfield, so I attended Mansfield Technical College and started a course on mining engineering. I was trained on things like coal dust explosions. Then my father died and I had to leave college. I came back to London and got a job in a firm that made scientific instruments.

I always had loved the cinema and thought, "Ah, well, I'm not really interested all that much in scientific instruments", so I applied for a job as rewind boy at the ABC cinema in Holloway Road, the Savoy. And my first job was actually to play the records. I wasn't allowed to touch any film. We used to have two turntables running 78 records and my first job was to put on the record selection before the cinema opened. Also, to actually scrub floors as well was expected of you in those days. The chiefs wouldn't let you near their projectors for a long, long time. That would have been 1945.

There was a shortage of projectionists as such, because most of them were called up for national service, although during the War it was considered to be a slightly "restricted" occupation by the Ministry of Labour because they had to keep some projectionists back. In this particular box were people who were medically unfit for national service, got exempted. I was there for about a year, just at the end of the war, sufficient to be around when the cinema just down the road, the Gaumont Holloway, actually had a flying bomb, a V1, landing inside it. In those days, after the War had been going on for a few years, they used to just put a slide up on the screen saying "There is an air raid in progress". People got so used to air raids that they didn't even bother going out.

In those days it was very good value for money. We used to give them two feature films, an interest short, newsreel and trailers. What used to annoy me intensely as a trainee was that I used to run most of the second feature but the chief always used to come in and run the newsreel and the bits and pieces, the interesting bits, and then go away again. The slog was always left up to the seconds and the thirds because the chiefs were above actually showing films - they were always down in the boiler house or something like that. The chief was responsible for his boilers, his plenum plant, air conditioning, everything electrical, secondary batteries, everything. It was his responsibility.

Even the lighting in the auditorium?

Everything. I always remember that the fitting in the Savoy was a great big chandelier and it was hand wound down and it used to take us two hours. It was all hand. It was a massive, great glass thing. We used to lamp it up not that often but it was hard work and it used to take most of the morning to wind it down, clean it and lamp it up and wind it back up again.

Do you remember when you first got your hand on films?

Yes, it was quite an experience to actually handle film because, in those days, we used to actually make hand splices. They wouldn't even pay for a machine to make a splice of a film so you used to get quite expert at actually making a hand splice. It was a work of art to actually make splices that did not come apart in projection because it was all nitrate in those days. We were always having fires. We used to blow them out. It was nothing to have a little gate fire in those days

but it was all fairly new stock so it wasn't a problem.

There were rules about staffing levels because of the fire risk?

In 1909 there was a Cinematograph Act as a result of a major fire and the rules were laid down that there should be a senior projectionist on duty and it was permitted to have a second person within immediate call. So most projection rooms, which were always high up in the building, had a staff room and toilet locally so you were more or less self-contained. You didn't want to go out because you had so many stairs to walk up and down, so you went up in the morning and very seldom came down again. The hours and the working conditions, of course, are not what they are today. We used to do a six day week and have one day off and occasionally get an evening off if the chief was in a good mood. But it was extremely long hours in those days.

What made you leave the Savoy?

I thought to myself I would like to further my career and I went to work in the Gaumont in the Haymarket. And I was the third projectionist there.

As a West End house, was that any different from working at Holloway?

Yes, it was. For example, you had extended runs. We used to work a shift pattern and that was mainly on a six-week run that a film stayed for in the West End in those days. I can remember running *The Wicked Lady* for six weeks, films like that, because it was a Gaumont house so it ran the Gainsborough movies a lot.

But as for projection standards, I've seen everything go wrong in the West End as much as anywhere else. I actually saw one chap change over a projector without any film in it. So everything that's gone wrong, I've seen.

We used to play jokes on the new rewind boys. We used to send the second to another cinema to get Technicolor carbons. There is a joke because it was the same for black-and-white as for Technicolor.

I left in 1947 to do national service in the RAF. I was very fortunate. We weren't paid very much money in those days, 28 shillings a week, but I was very lucky in that there was a camp cinema and I used to occasionally help out the manager/operator. They were called Astra cinemas and he didn't always want to show the movies, so I used to get paid for running the movie for him in the evenings, which supplemented my RAF pay for a while. Then I got shipped to Berlin and I served on the airlift for eighteen months.

At the end of my service career, which was 1949, I decided I'd like to go back into the cinema, so I got a job as a second operator. You know how they used to have the grades of operator: there was a chief, co-chief, a senior second, junior second, senior third, junior third, a rewind boy.

And everybody learned the trade on the job?

There were a couple of courses. Gaumont had one at the old Holborn Empire, which got bombed. They used it as a training school for a few years but I only went there for about two days.

The Gaumont Palace Camden Town in 1937 with 2,742 seats (the circle is now the main auditorium of the Parkway Cinema)

I went to work at the Gaumont North Finchley as a second projectionist. The chief projectionist was named Pat Dunk. I stayed there for about nine months and then was transferred to the Gaumont at Camden Town, which is now the Parkway Cinema. It was a very large cinema in those days, beautifully equipped, and I stayed there for a while.

We used to have always two to a change-over. There is a change-over cue which is a round dot in the corner of the screen. And, because some projection rooms were about 150 feet away from the screen, we always used to put white paint alongside the cue dot. So one projectionist would be looking on the screen for the motor cues and one would be looking for the white paint on the side of the film. So the projectionist on the outgoing machine would cue the incoming machine by saying "Motor" and then "Over" was the cue.

One thing I did experience was "arc eyes" and that's a terrible thing to have. Carbon rods were rationed, during the War especially, so the chiefs used to make sure they burned every scrap of carbon rod they could possibly get out. There was always a stump end. It was like a cork tip of a cigarette.

There was always a bit at the end. Now, if you didn't gauge it right, you used to manually push it through, and if you looked too closely at the point of light you used to burn the retina and it was just like having sawdust in the eyes. You had to stay in a darkened room for a day. It was a common occurrence. We never had dark glasses or anything like that. You'd just open the arc door and bang it through with the back end of a screwdriver and keep it going.

And then we've had the take-ups go. If the take-up belt broke, you'd manually turn it. I've actually wound 2,000ft. of film like that for twenty minutes just to keep the film going. They wouldn't do it today but you just didn't stop in those days.

And in those days we used to have pea soupers and I've actually shown a film where I couldn't see the screen and we had to rely on those pieces of white paint to change-over because we couldn't see the picture. It happened at the National Film Theatre because there was that bad fog of '54 when it was real smog. We couldn't see the screen but we carried on.

In those days there was one standard gauge, one standard format, which was the Academy 3 by 4, aspect ratio 1.33 to 1. In those days you had one format, one ratio, one sound system. And the one lens stayed in the gate.

We did organ interludes at Finchley and Camden Town. We used to make rainfall effects and cloud effects and all that sort of thing during the organ interlude. And we used to put on the words of the song while the organist was playing. It didn't always work but sometimes it did. Somebody was always putting the slides on upside down and the wrong way round. Then occasionally you'd have a film with the bouncing ball, with the words on the ball. The chief would instruct you on how to use the Brenograph, the effects lantern.

The shows were extremely good value for one shilling or ninepence, I thought. You used to get four hours. A lot of people used to go there because they were kept warm. We had a fuel shortage in the Forties, just after the War. A lot of people used to go to the cinema to save heating their homes. They would be out from 6 to 10.30 and they'd go to bed and get up and go to work.

Working in a projection box must have been quite an isolated world, very enclosed.

A very, very isolated world. You were behind those portholes, those small apertures. And you used to have full houses - you'd have people in a 2,000-seater auditorium all chattering away - you could actually hear all this hub-bub going on - and then suddenly you pressed the house lights and all the chatter goes, they shut up, and the music would fade and you'd open the curtains and you'd play the censor and suddenly bring up either the Fox intro or the MGM. They were great.

The chief always used to view the film on Monday afternoons with the audience and set the volume levels. We used to have cue sheets. The sound was all set to one SMPTE standard and it didn't vary that much.

Didn't the volume level depend on the number of people in the auditorium?

You compensated a couple of fader points for the number of people that were in the house. So you knew if you had a fader setting of 6 - the dial is 0 to 10 - you would bring it up to 7 or 8 for a full house.

Your prints were usually in good condition.

Yes. Every print you ever had from RKO or MGM was finely checked and they used to, in those days, put an embossed stamp over the splices, so it would be "MGM" across to stop people cutting splices out.

Was everything so well rehearsed that things didn't go wrong?

Yes, everything went wrong. One of the old tricks of the trade: the chief said, "If you ever, ever put a wrong part on..." (and everybody's done it once) "always break the top loop and go for a white light because the audience will not remember that it was the wrong scene - they will think that it's a break."

Weren't they quite strict about things like that? Could it get you the sack?

Yes, in the circuit houses you'd go before a district engineer. There were no industrial tribunals in those days. And if you made too many mistakes, they always had methods - because they could ship you to a circuit house miles away, they would offer you a job that you just couldn't take. That was one way they controlled you.

Did you meet your wife in a cinema?

Yes. She was the cashier at the Gaumont Finchley. Which is always happening in life - most people meet through the course of their work. We met and then we married within the year and then we had a child who is in the business. We had a problem of finding somewhere to live so we moved to Southend on Sea. I got a job at the ABC cinema, which was the Rivoli and is now the Cannon or MGM.

While I was there, I got a telephone call from this chap, Pat Dunk, who said to me did I want a job as a projectionist at the National Film Theatre. And I said, "What's the

National Film Theatre?" And he said that it was the Telekinema built for the Festival of Britain, and would I like to come and be the junior second. I didn't have an interview. So I decided that I would take the job and I started on 17 October 1952, one week before it opened as the National Film Theatre.

The opening night of the NFT, that was an interesting night. The programme was a sort of history of cinema and all the equipment we had we used. Derek Prouse, who is a film

The first NFT, the former Telekinema

critic, and Lindsay Anderson were either side of the stage and they each had a script and introduced. We started off with a silent film and went through the whole, ending with the latest four-track magnetic sound film. The great names of cinema were there, people like John Ford and René Clair. And Princess Margaret.

And Lindsay had this idea that a technician should be introduced to the audience. They didn't think that much of that. So Lindsay said, "Well, if you don't have a technician, I'm not going to do the show." So in the end they gave way. So I had to go on the stage and get my picture of Waterloo Bridge which I've got.

When you first started at the NFT, what was it like? What were your impressions?

It was a slightly different world from what I'd been used to.

I always remember I got told off for cutting the head numbers off *The Man with a Movie Camera*. It comes up "1" and I thought "What's this doing here?", so I snipped. I destroyed it.

Vertov re-edited by Charles Beddow!

Pat Dunk was the first chief. He went. Within a year two chiefs had left and the second. It was at the time that ITV started and a lot of projectionists went to work for ITV companies as telecine operators, etc. So there was a chief's job available. So I said were they going to offer it to me, because if they weren't I was going to go to television as well. So I became the chief projectionist at the NFT when I was 24.

We still ran three-dimensional films. We started off running them at lunchtime but it never worked. The Festival was successful but we carried on after the Festival. A lot of people don't realise that the NFT nearly closed in '54. The audiences went right down and it was a very expensive operation. It was just as well they had the Royal Festival Hall there because if the Royal Festival Hall was ever full we'd get

Charles Beddow (left) in the projection box of the original NFT, with Pat Dunk

the overflow. I don't think we would have survived otherwise.

We used to have problems with print supply because of the nitrate problem. They didn't have the money to print up. So we used to have a 16mm print and we used to do crazy things because there was only one [16mm] machine in the

The purpose-built National Film Theatre with its main entrance on the riverside (the area since extended to incorporate the present restaurant and bar)

projection room - we couldn't get two machines in that box, there was only an aperture where the television projector had been. We used to change over to 35 [mm] for five minutes while we re-laced the 16mm up. Just because they couldn't afford to print a [whole] 35 copy.

We were only temporary there and the NFT in 1957 moved over from the Telekinema to the [new purpose-built] NFT and it was very successful. The worst programme we ever did was Open Cinema. This was a television festival. We ran a series of television films and nobody came to them, absolutely nobody. People just would not pay to go and see stuff that they could see free on television.

Were there certain films in the Fifties that people flocked to see?

I always remember *The Wild One*, the Brando movie. I know we ran a special performance of that to help pay for the seating in the NFT. It was the staff's contribution toward the seating in NFT 1.

In the Fifties and Sixties I think the NFT was really good. The nicest thing I ever heard was that somebody once said that they were never conscious of projection. I think that is the ideal. If you are conscious of projection, there is something wrong.

Mo Heard

Mo Heard, born in 1940, went into acting as a career and is now in charge of the Actors' Company at the Museum of the Moving Image. She is also interviewed in Being There and Film Talk.

I went to drama school and obviously intended to have a long career in the theatre. During holidays at drama school, a friend of mine and I, we got a job throughout the summer selling ice creams in the Plaza in Lower Regent Street. It was the first time that I'd encountered an advanced booking film: it was *The Counterfeit Traitor* with William Holden and Lilli Palmer and it had an interval. It wasn't a continuous performance. We sold ice creams at the beginning and the end of the film and in the interval. And when you were in the circle, it was absolutely terrifying because you had to be in your position at the front of the circle before the lights went up, so you would have to go down all these vertiginous steps with this heavy tray in front of you so that you couldn't see the steps in the dark while the film was going on. When you got there, the wall at the front of the circle seemed exceedingly low and you had to turn round and face all these people and you really felt you were going to fall over the edge. And then, of course, as the lights went up they all rushed at you - "Could I have a bag of nuts?"...

And because we were there six weeks and the film was on the whole time and in the first half and the second we had nothing else to do, we would sit in the back row and we watched *The Counterfeit Traitor* until we knew

The Counterfeit Traitor: a premiere season at the Plaza Lower Regent Street in 1962

every single line of dialogue and it was a three hour film and they all had German accents. We used to fall about laughing going home, coming out with all these lines. But the other interesting thing was that, seeing the film so often, we spotted lots of continuity faults. I think we counted about one hundred continuity faults, like where in one shot he had his hanky sticking out of his pocket and in the next shot he didn't. And there was a mirror shot in a big room: there was a big, ornate mirror over the mantlepiece and then the next shot the frame was still there but they'd taken the mirror out so it was just the wall behind it. Things like that you

The vertiginous circle of the Plaza (1926 photograph)

wouldn't ever have spotted the first time out. And that was fascinating.

I became an usherette at the NFT in 1964, just before they went down to near the Tate Gallery, the Millbank Tower. I just saw the job advertised and came along and worked there. They were refurbishing the NFT and when we came back I usheretted a couple of years. Being in the NFT and seeing two different films a night, fourteen a week, was just a continuation of my interest.

While I was working at the NFT, I was in a Hammer film which sank without trace. It was made as a follow-up to *One Million Years B.C.* It was a film called *Prehistoric Women* and I was in that as a prehistoric woman wearing a sort of woolley bikini. I used to have to get up at five o'clock in the morning

Mo Heard is in the group of dark-haired women in this shot from Prehistoric Women *(1968). It was released in Britain as* Slave Girls *(1968) and starred Martine Beswick and Michael Latimer*

and go off to Pinewood and have dark brown make-up put all over me and then I had to get back for the second house, the 8.30 house. I didn't have time to shower all the stuff off, so I used to just wash my face down to my neck and the rest of my body was covered with brown make-up. I used to put on the navy blue dress, pick up my torch, and off I went to the 8.30 house. I loved usheretting. I was terribly assertive with my torch. Then I used to help out in the box-office and then I became the assistant box-office manager.

I've worked at the NFT on and off since about 1964. I've used the experience I've had working in theatre, having been an actor and also administrative work in publishing and running acting classes and employing directors and people like that - I set up the actors' company at the Museum of the Moving Image and now I'm company manager.

I don't think that you have any atmosphere now going to the cinema. What I remember from going to the cinema as a child is that fantastic atmosphere and the dreams and the glamour and the difference of the reality that you came from and being in all those amazing cinemas with all the plush and gilt. Fantastic!

The former Gaumont in the King's Road, Chelsea, as the Odeon (since converted to Habitat with the Chelsea Cinema in the old circle)

Aine O'Halloran

Aine O'Halloran, born in 1950, was part of the Irish community in Pimlico as a child. She usheretted briefly at a Chelsea cinema and now works for the British Film Institute's distribution department. She also appears in Being There.

I started work when I was fourteen. When I was fifteen I was working in this office. I never had enough money so I worked as an usherette. That would be the Gaumont in the King's Road. It only lasted about three weeks because it was so god-awful and so badly paid, but I can remember the films I saw in those three weeks as an usherette when you see them every night for a week. And that's when I became much more involved in the film and I suddenly realised films were quite important. Because I came in at six and it was halfway through, I saw the ends before I saw the beginning. It was a bit bad - one was a comedy and I kept laughing before the thing happened.

But you hated being an usherette.

All the usherettes were treated as if they were some kind of lepers who had happened in for the evening and needed to be spoken to as cretins from the minute they set their feet in till the minute they went home. And they had this horrid brown nylon overall thing to wear which was really hot and uncomfortable.

So you had that and you were badly paid and they changed your hours without so much as a by-your-leave, but the worst thing was the way this manager, who personally I thought had the brains of a rubber plant, would talk to me as though I was a complete cretin.

You always had to sell ice-creams as well and I could not bear to stand at the front with this thing around my neck. I would find every excuse not to have to do my turn at selling ice-creams. It was uncomfortable, it was humiliating standing there with this great silly tray on me pulling me down, making me look foolish.

But they were well staffed, I'll say that. There were always two of you. You don't see that many staff these days. So if it was really busy you could handle it. And the slow bits I didn't mind because I used to flick my torch around at people in the back row to catch sight of them. A girl friend I worked with, she would sit the other side and we would flash across and then we would flash back because we'd spotted a couple we knew were going to be up to no good, so we would have a little flick round at them. It stopped the boredom.

It only lasted three weeks because I was sacked. The manager started in on one of these lectures one day after I thought he'd handled a situation really badly, so I thought I ought to tell him. And the situation was one where there was a suspected fire and I had an understanding that if you were to go around shouting fire in a cinema it would be a fairly dangerous thing. We used to have these lectures once a week about what the password is and what you would do should there be a fire, and he found a fire in a wastepaper bin and he was running up and down the corridor shouting "There's a bin on fire. There's a bin on fire." I said, "I don't think you should be doing that." He told me I was insolent and I didn't fit in with the company's policy. That was the end of my cinema usheretting career but it did teach me to watch the film and not to be snogging.

What sort of tastes did you develop in films when you started choosing them?

I don't know if it's to do with the subliminal effects of

snogging for hours on end, but I developed this taste for very long, slow films.

Film Talk

 In this section, talk about stars flows more freely than talk about individual films or genres. We glean something of the influence of cinema-going on the way people behaved and talked. We hear about tastes and find a general preference for Hollywood films but with nods to particular British figures from Old Mother Riley to Stewart Granger. British films are found to be too class-ridden, too stiff-upper-lip, compared to films from Hollywood. British stars evoke envy and empathy, setting up contradictory notions of stars-as-special and stars-as-ordinary, the kind of people you might see on the street.

 The reminiscences confirm the notion that many picturegoers went regularly to particular cinemas regardless of what was showing, that they looked out for films with the stars they liked, and it is the stars that are remembered more than most individual pictures.

 Also recalled is the role of the weekly large circulation fan magazines like Picturegoer and Picture Show, of the annuals like Film Review, and of star photographs (sold in shops, or sometimes autographed and sent by the stars themselves) - all part of the process by which mass interest in the cinema was cultivated and sustained.

 Then there was the role of the specialised and art cinemas. French and other foreign films, with both a more mature and a more sensational approach to sex and other adult themes, offered an alternative to the British and American output. Some French films like *The Wages of Fear*, *Mon Oncle* and *And Woman…Was Created* were widely shown outside the specialised West End cinemas. But most were largely confined to the Academy, Cameo-Poly, Curzon Mayfair and other art houses, perhaps to be selectively shown in suburban Classics and other independent cinemas at a later date. The National Film Theatre offered both a chance to savour obscure foreign films and catch revivals of Hollywood and British classics.

Fred Creasey (right) and Bill Halle (left) in the French cinema section of the Museum of the Moving Image

Fred Creasey and Bill Halle

Fred Creasey and Bill Halle, born in 1931 and 1912 respectively, are lifelong friends who share a passion for painting and seeing films. Bill Halle's recollections also appear in Being There.

Are there films you remember from when you were six?

BH: Yes. Sessue Hayakawa, the Japanese actor, a very strong man. One of the things I wasn't allowed to see was he used to brand his women and the branding scene was always concealed from me by Mother's hat. And I particularly remember *The Four Horsemen of the Apocalypse* coming to Broadstairs and the sensation it caused. It was really the beginning of a cinema explosion. I'm sure Broadstairs was never the same again. I remember my sister and mother talking about it in hushed tones so I wouldn't hear. But, of course, I did hear and I wanted to see it. My mother must have gone through a lot of strategies to keep me from seeing it. I never saw it.

In those days they had different classes of cinemas. There was the sort of society cinema which only showed society films, as they called it, with ballroom scenes and that sort of thing. And people having dinners as opposed to eating fish and chips in the other films. Of course, as they were silent films you didn't realise that all these women who got up in evening dress were talking with American accents. You only had the titles and you assumed they were talking with an

English accent. And it was a great shock when talkies came and they had American accents.

What did you think of Garbo?

BH: We had had people like Pola Negri and along that line, and Lili Damita who was another one who was rather startling. But Garbo was extraordinarily different from anyone who had been before. A lot of shop girls used to go together to these cinemas and chatter. I used to go and sit behind them to hear what they said. Some of them thought she was horrible. Their favourite was Antonio Moreno who was playing the hero in *The Temptress* and they felt she wasn't worthy of him. But others raved about her. They were absolutely divided whether they liked her or hated her and that made her sensational.

Was it a male/female thing? Did men tend to like Garbo?

BH: I think at first it was largely female. She seemed to exude something that no actress before her had done. Even Lya de Putti had been quite different - she was a German actress very much to the fore then. In fact, we saw all the best German films.

Your mother and sister were very cinema-minded?

BH: Yes. My grandmother just refused to go. She was of a past generation and refused to accept the cinema. But my mother was in between - she was slightly horrified by it but very much attracted. We used to go a lot, once a week, and we used the better cinema at Clifton, the right side of Margate - the Casino. They had all the best films.

Was there a sense that certain films were suitable for children and certain films not suitable?

BH: There were. The suitable ones were serials and those were the ones I went for. *Fu Manchu* going on week after week, and Pearl White being tied to the rail in front of a train. They always ended on a high note, so you came back again. You got quite a long programme, you always got the Pathe Gazette and you always got a comedy and the serial and then the big picture. You expected that and every cinema gave it. But the big pictures weren't so long then. The average one was about an hour.

Can you remember the music? Was it a single piano or did they have an orchestra?

BH: Several of them did. There was an awfully nice cinema of a higher class at Herne Bay, on the front, called the Blue Domes. I always loved that name, wanted to go there. And it used to have these society films, and Betty Compson was the chief actress in those. I remember my sister going to see a film called *Woman to Woman*. I wasn't allowed to see it. They had an orchestra - a fair-sized one, I believe. And only the very small ones had a piano.

Fred, you went to the cinema quite a lot during the War?

FC: Yes, I think that's why I have a particular liking for British films. My earliest youth was very much connected with British films, because as I grew up during the War there was an awful lot of British films around - British wartime movies like *The Way to the Stars* and *The Way Ahead*.

BH: I loved those. Superb films. You could feel right part of them. David Niven as an officer.

FC: There was a whole series of British actors of that time.

BH: William Hartnell - he was always the sergeant major.

FC: The first European movies I got to like - when I was doing national service there was very much a Cocteau thing in the air, and I must have seen *Les Enfants Terribles* at least half a dozen times, maybe more.

So you were a frequenter of art cinemas just after the War?

FC: I suppose so. It was when I was doing national service I suddenly became aware that the blokes I was with used to talk

William Hartnell (rear) as the Sergeant Major in The Way Ahead
*(1944) with Raymond Huntley, John Laurie, Jimmy Hanley, James
Donald and Stanley Holloway*

about people like Jean Cocteau. Names like Sartre were just coming into being. At first, it was a sort of intellectual snobbery about it all: Continental films were okay things to go to. But I really did like them as well. I still feel a lot of those old French movies were great.

Why did you like them?

FC: I have an idea it was partly that they explored notions about sex for a start. I don't mean sex in a kind of "X" explicit way. They were often people involved in sexual situations. There was a passionate thing about a lot of French movies which was obviously not a British tradition. The stiff British upper lip. And I thought they treated sex in a very lovely way. And another reason I liked them was because at the time I was very into painting. Painting was a French thing - you'd actually sometimes see people in French films talking about painting seriously.

BH: It was the dialogue one liked, too. It was actually intelligent dialogue.

FC: There was a kind of intelligent, intellectual quality about the dialogue. In *Brief Encounter*, the bit in the

restaurant where Trevor Howard's asking Celia Johnson about her husband and I think there's a palm court trio in the background. And he asks her if her husband likes music and she says no and he says "That's good", as if anybody who likes music would be really suspect. It's anti-intellectual. Whereas French films, they embrace intellectuals. So often they were set in places where there was a vaguely art or arty connection. Somebody like Cocteau was not just somebody who made films - you associated him with poetry and you associated him with people like Picasso. There was a whole poetic thing. But as you say the dialogue, very often, was very very intelligent dialogue.

BH: Yes, and very natural at the same time - quite opposite from the dialogue you had in American films.

Did you go to American films as well?

BH: No. I had a highbrow phase and I wouldn't go to American films and consequently I missed an enormous lot. But I dragged someone who liked American films to see *The Wages of Fear*, which I thought was terrific. That was at the Academy. He said there were American films as good and I

Cocteau's Les Enfants Terribles (1949), *directed by
Jean-Pierre Melville with Nicole Stéphane and Edouard
Dhermitte*

wouldn't believe him, but actually there probably were. Some American films are very very good. A film like *The Postman Always Rings Twice* I thought was an exciting film, and *Sunset Boulevard* I thought was a splendid film.

FC: As you say, there was a kind of highbrow thing knocking around at the time and one liked things like *Sunset Boulevard* because there was a highbrow quality about that, partly because it had those old stars in it and again in that the dialogue is very intelligent. Funnily enough, it was in the Fifties when I was in my highbrow stage that I remember

Charles Vanel and Yves Montand (driving) in The Wages of Fear *(1953)*

getting into one or two American films and thinking they were actually quite good. There were qualities about some of the French films which we liked because they had qualities of the Hollywood film as well. *The Wages of Fear* was very exciting. It was the one about these lorry drivers. They're all in this South American place. They haven't got any money and they're given this chance of driving these lorries full of gelignite, and the whole film is concerned with the drive. Some of them get killed and some don't, and there's bits where they have to drive across particularly nasty roads and the dynamite or whatever it is might get jerked about and blow them up. I think I saw it at the Academy, although it did have a wider showing, that one.

BH: People were against French films with subtitles outside the West End.

FC: I remember seeing a film by Clouzot who made *The Wages of Fear*. It was called *The Fiends*. It was really very scary.

BH: That was shown at the Cameo-Poly in Upper Regent Street.

FC: I saw it in Upper Regent Street. And there was a great publicity thing associated with it, even though it was a French film. I think they were trying to get a French film across as a popular film for English audiences. It certainly was incredibly scary where the guy gets up out of the bath at the end.

Were you in a group of people who talked about films?

BH: No. Funnily enough, I wasn't. I had nobody to talk to. The people I knew were all into American films. I realised after a while it was hopeless trying to interest them in French films. I really was crazy about French films and then it kind of died away. The quality of them slowly went down somehow.

FC: There was a heavily romantic quality about them from the end of the War up until the Fifties. Then French films changed when people like Godard came on the scene and started making these heavily intellectual films. I remember seeing some of the early Godard films. But the one thing I couldn't understand about Godard was why he had this passion for American films because at the time I despised American films. I couldn't understand why he liked gangster films and he didn't try to make French films.

DON'T BE A FIEND!
Don't reveal even to your best friends the startling end of
THE FIENDS
("Les Diaboliques")
CERT 'X'
H. G. ("Wages of Fear")
Clouzot's greatest thriller
starring
SIMONE SIGNORET · VERA CLOUZOT
You must see it from the start
Programmes at 12.30, 3.05, 5.40, 8.15
CAMEO-POLY
OXFORD CIRCUS   LANgham 1744

Did Continental films have a sleazy appeal?

FC: It was true. I remember Vi, my sister, talking about a French film, and it's a memory I have from when I was in my teens. She'd been up to the West End to see this film, and I remember her describing it to my mother. She didn't put it quite in those words but obviously the couple had had sex, and you saw the bottom half of the woman, you saw her dress fall to the floor - a classic shot, one of the great conventions. She thought it was a bit nasty.

But there was a period when you tended to get a quite good French movie and a kind of nudie movie at the same cinema. One of my favourite stories about turning up to see a Godard film, *Une Femme Mariée*, and turning up at the end of this film where you saw lots of female bums disappearing into the distance. It was set in a nudist colony and the cinema was absolutely packed. I had a feeling Godard had suddenly become incredibly popular but at the end of this nudie film everyone walked out. I was about the only one left for *Une Femme Mariée*

Len England

Len England, born in 1920, has retired to Wales after a career in market research. He was part of Mass Observation's well-known large-scale investigation of everyday life in the Thirties and Forties and became a director of that organisation after the War. He also appears in Being There.

As a child, I was a desperate reader of Picturegoer every week. I became fascinated by cinema in the same way I had been before with magazines and things when I collected not only the Tiny Tims but the Beanos and the Dandys and I ran a library from my mother's kitchen.

I loved the sort of thing my mother loved - *Victoria the Great* with Anna Neagle, and Deanna Durbin of course. She used to hate being frightened and I'm surprised I even saw *King Kong* in the Thirties. I'm sure I didn't see it with her. I was eighteen by then so I would see my own films.

I don't recall many art films from those days although the Benjamin Brittens and Audens were writing posh documentaries. By the end of 1940 I'd seen all the big ones. But the other big documentaries were coming over, like *Men of the Lightship*. Some of the propaganda films were obvious propaganda like *Fire Over England*, and some of them were much more subtle like *Lightship*, where the Germans bomb the lightship and the men die when they get to shore. It was a very moving film. I went to see Jean Gabin in his *Quai des Brumes* and that was when I started going to the Academy. I suspect I was weaned away from the Astoria and my mother between 1937 and 1939 and started seeing those films then. But certainly until my later teens I was a Hollywood addict and an unashamed one.

Did you have a preference for American over British films in the Thirties?

In the Thirties, yes. They were making all the Anna Neagle films which I though were very nice but most of the great films were coming from Hollywood. My guess is that there were a limited number of very good British films, like those of Korda, who came over and started making *Henry VIII* and all those. But, for every one good British film, there were four or five good Hollywood films, and by "good" I mean entertaining.

People like George Formby only started in the War. Jessie Matthews was very good - she appeared in stage shows before the War. The big films were things like *Victoria the Great* and then the Korda films.

Deanna Durbin

What about Gracie Fields? Did you like her?

Not very much. She was common. I think one got more and more to like her until at the end you got *Sing As You Go*, but her early films were much too common and North Country for me - I was too posh for them.

So you had rather a Southern and genteel approach?

Yes, I was brought up very genteel, not unpleasantly, but no, you wouldn't like Northern humour. You wouldn't particularly like Cockney humour. One associated Wally Patch as the eternal Cockney. Life was very different then. Claude Dampier was a comedian before the War, and he had a woman in the audience called Mrs. Gibson who he used to talk to like Edna Everage, and apparently on the radio in 1935 or 1936 he said, "I'll come and squeeze your oranges, Mrs. Gibson," and they cut him off the radio for a year for being filthy. Incredible.

Do any particular war films stand out in your memory?

The Way to the Stars - Michael Redgrave repeating the John Pudney poem, "Little Johnny Head in the Air", Rosamund John keeping a stiff upper lip. A bloody good film. I did love Bernard Miles - *Tawny Pipit*, which was an escape film, a gorgeous film. Most of the wartime films were tight upper lip showing everybody their good side and not their bad side. I still cannot believe that Deborah Kerr had an affair with Burt

A big film of the Thirties: Anna Neagle in Victoria the Great

Lancaster or whoever she did have after the War, because Deborah Kerr was so curt all the way through the War, like Olivia de Havilland was, and you couldn't believe them having affairs with anybody. Now she admits it all, it really is shattering, it makes you feel very old. But it was that sort of

image - Deborah Kerr is a case in point, because *Major Barbara* was before the War or very close to the War and then she moved onto the wartime films still as the stiff-upper-lip lady. Anna Neagle was exactly the same and very good. You went to American films for different reasons - English films to be basically uplifted and American films to enjoy yourself.

Anna Neagle

Denis Norden

Denis Norden, born in 1922, is the well-known radio and television personality. His reminiscences also appear in Being There and Working There.

I can't talk for the whole of Britain because I'm purely a Londoner. We watched these American films uncomprehendingly. We would take in expressions incomprehensible to us, like "I can't go to the Prom", "I'm not wearing your frat pin", "Oh, well, pour me a Scotch on the rocks". We had no idea what "on the rocks" meant - we had visions of Grace Darling going out. And then these campus films with American football - we had no idea what we were doing there, but we knew it was terribly important because it was the final game, the plot depended on it, and people talked about being behind the eight ball and having two strikes against him, and "I didn't get to first base with her", but we somehow learnt it simply by its context. We never used the vocabulary which is what is different today when these new phrases come into the language. Today people adopt them and use them. We - the young people of that time - somehow didn't embrace them. You went along with them but you didn't for a moment think of ever using that phrase.

Not even when you were in your peer group?

No. You'd never say "I'll take a raincheck", even though we had a misty idea of what a raincheck might be. There's no such thing. There still isn't in England.

Yet you read people were complaining that American films were corrupting the English language.

The people who complained - maybe the top .001 per cent - would write letters in Horizon and Penguin New Writing maybe, but not in John Bull or Picture Post or any of the popular papers or magazines of the time. Yes, you'd get a

C. A. Lejeune, a film critic, who would occasionally launch an attack on the Americanisms, but it was in a sense unjustified in that they didn't really get in the language.

But films did have some deeper influence?

My generation learned how to be human beings from films. You learned how to smoke, for example, from films. You learned how to hold a cigarette. You learned that only characters that played untrustworthy, very low class, smoked like that [*demonstrating*]. To be suave, to be William Powell, to be Franchot Tone, you held it like that. The great scene in *Now Voyager* with Paul Henreid and Bette Davis where he lights two cigarettes - well, the number of burnt lips perpetrated all over England! You do that and the girl says no, and you're left with two cigarettes on the go. But that went all the way - eating, walking, what you wore.

My ambition for years was to have a white dinner jacket or a long camel-coloured coat which I would put round my shoulders without putting my arms through my sleeve, because that was easy confidence - that was my objective correlative for easy confidence. So, in a sense, everything you learned about being a unit in modern society came from films.

We had a lot of wrong impressions as well. I was most disappointed when I came to shave because if you watch shaving on films they do this, "I'll be there in a minute, honey." I thought that's all shaving was. I thought there was something wrong with me, doing this and going over and over and over. And driving: because all driving shots were back projection in those days, the actors would sit in this mock-up car and they'd go like this, so I thought that when you drove you kept jiggling the wheel. My first car was a Morris Oxford, and I remember a time when the driving instructor said, "What are you doing!"

Do you remember which films were really big hits when you were at the Trocadero?

Old Mother Riley. In South London, Old Mother Riley and her daughter Kitty, a whole series of rubbishy British films they made, you could not go wrong with them. There was a series of films made by Mancunian Films with Norman Evans

Arthur Lucan with Kitty McShane in Old Mother Riley in Society *(1940)*

Below - Mickey Rooney as Andy with Cecelia Parker and Lewis Stone in Andy Hardy Gets Spring Fever *(1939)*

and Frank Randle - they were a great hit. There was *The Falcon* - that was a series of films in which George Sanders, and before him George Sanders' brother, Tom Conway, played this kind of figure like the Saint, the gentleman crook who actually solves murders and comes to the rescue of people. Enormously successful.

The Andy Hardy films I saw over and over again. It's only looking back you realise why you saw them, because they had Mickey Rooney and Judy Garland, and Judy Garland was somebody for the ages - she was simply a great performer. There were many, many like her. Nowadays she stands out. People didn't bother with all the mini Judy Garlands there were around then, and there were many like her, and you didn't realise she stood out so much.

People like Laurel and Hardy, for example, who have now become kind of cultural icons, they were just fillers in those days. People would get up and go when Laurel and Hardy shorts came on because that was what we call part of the wines and spirits - they were just filling.

Clifford Gentle

Clifford Gentle, born in 1926, became an actor, director and writer under the professional name of Clifford John Williams, and likes to see classic films at the National Film Theatre. He is also featured in Being There.

Marlene Dietrich in Knight Without Armour *(1937)*

Did your mother talk to you about films?

Oh, in the evenings, yes. And some she insisted on coming. She wouldn't think of me going by myself to *Things to Come*, for example.

Because she was worried you'd get frightened?

She'd heard about this film and it was about sleeping sickness or something like that and she'd heard it wasn't very nice. And I said I wanted to see it but she said we'll go together and she held my hand throughout. I wasn't a bit nervous.

Maybe she was. At school, did teachers ever talk about cinema or was it something they regarded as a bit vulgar?

Not vulgar but kind of a waste of time. Some of them really disapproved. I remember a lady teacher telling me no good would come to me. I couldn't understand what she meant but I remember the words: "No good will come to you if you go to picture palaces." Which, of course, made it more glamorous than ever. You thought, "I've been to a picture palace, one of those wicked places."

I was always getting crushes on various movie stars. When I was six or seven, I adored Marlene Dietrich and I'm afraid that I did sit through *Knight Without Armour* several times, then I desperately wanted to see it again that week and there was no hope of getting another ninepence from Mother - I couldn't say to her, "Can I go to the pictures again?" And I'm afraid I was somewhat outrageous about that because he looked a pleasant-enough young man, he looked as if there would be no trouble, and I said, "Excuse me, could you take me in?" He said, "Yes, of course." I said, "I haven't got any money." He said, "That's all right. I'll pay for you." So he bought my ticket. I felt somewhat scarlet nevertheless - but I saw *Knight Without Armour* again, twice, so I saw it four times that week.

When her films were on, I used to do little stickers, tiny little stickers. I used to put what the film was, Dietrich in something, Astoria, May 19th or whatever the date was, and - I don't know why - then I went and put one of those in every single phone box I passed. I put one just where the telephone was.

I wrote an essay once. We were supposed to do a short story and I wrote this story about Marlene - I think, in *Desire*. I called the story *Desire* and I really did get quite a severe telling off from the headmaster. He said, "It isn't healthy for a young boy to be infatuated" - it was the first time I'd heard the word - "with an older woman." And, of course, it made it all the more glamorous.

Did you read about her? Did you buy fan magazines?

Yes. We used to have Picturegoer, Film Weekly which was rather grander, and Picture Show - that had much more Hollywood gossip. The gents, I didn't come on to the gents. I enjoyed them but it was always these elegant ladies who turned me on.

What about Gracie Fields?

Oh yes, I liked her.

Did you like George Formby?

I loved George Formby. Oh, and what I adored was Old Mother Riley. I used to drive Mother mad by imitating her at home.

What was the big appeal of Old Mother Riley?

A link with pantomime. "Oh, go to the foot of the stairs."

What does it mean?

You go to the foot of our stairs. It means you're on your dignity. Because we don't want to speak. You give just one look more and you're upstairs. On the streets, the neighbours, because you've got steps up to our house.

Because George Formby used to say it quite a lot as well.

It was very well known. Mother often said it.

Did people in the South like people like George Formby?

The working class did. The cockney ones did.

You liked melodramas?

The historical melodramas, like *Elizabeth and Essex* - I saw that in Northampton. I was evacuated.

With the historical film, was it the kind of glamour of going in to another world that you liked and did it make you read about the subject?

It did. That's why I'm always grateful to them. Because I virtually had no education, because at the school I was at, at Brixton, I learnt absolutely nothing. I just remember noise in the classroom and being very unhappy and wishing I could learn something, so I read avidly at home, all the time. And I think I took every play out of Brixton library in my early teens. I loved things like, because I suppose it took you to another world, like *The Three Musketeers*.

You went for musicals in a big way?

Swing Time, I remember. I was staying with a friend of Mother's who had a pub over at Ealing Broadway and her mother had a pass to the cinema. This daughter was called Beryl. Beryl and I went every day to *Swing Time*. And then used to dance home through the streets.

What other stars did you like in the Thirties?

Gladys George. Wasn't she splendid? A very good supporting actress. She played Madame Du Barry in *Marie Antoinette* and she played the nightclub woman in *The Roaring Twenties*. She has the marvellous last line. Cagney's shot and she is cradling him. You just see the back of a policeman and he says, "Who was he?" and she just looks up

"He used to be a big shot": Gladys George cradles James Cagney in The Roaring Twenties *(1939)*

and says, "He used to be a big shot."

But it's funny. When I was on duty, on watch in an aircraft carrier, I looked out the window, and you'd think of these lines and you'd half imagine the cameras turning because it's the same kind of aura. I think it was something cinema did - even the things which at one time might have seemed ordinary and insignificant have their own significance. That's one of the things that cinema's done.

Did the cinema directly influence the way people behaved, do you think?

When I was going to the Far East, we came up from Chatham and we were going to get the train to Portsmouth from Waterloo and I said to the petty officer, "How long are we going to wait?" And he said, "About two-and-a half hours." I rang up my girlfriend (who's now dead, bless her heart). I said, could she come and see me on the station. She saw me off. Muriel was standing on the station and we did the full thing - a long, long kiss on the station, all the sailors

watching - and the train was pulling out, she put her hanky... She said it was strange, it was a mixture of acting and yet it wasn't, because who knows if she would see me again and what would happen.

Is it true that, when girls kissed, they always stood on their toes and that came from the movies?

Yes, and sometimes they said they heard music. My sister-in-law, said with one American she kissed during the War she definitely heard music. But I'm sure that was the influence of the movies. And you did it half-conscious to the camera, as I used to stand on the deck like Garbo in *Queen Christina* - except, of course, the wind's blowing the wrong way.

"The wind's blowing the wrong way": Garbo at the end of Queen Christina *(1933)*

Undersea Kingdom (1936): C. Montagu Shaw prepares to attack hero Ray "Crash" Corrigan while he is preoccupied with one of the Volkites...

Norman Cobden

Norman Cobden, born in 1932, lives in Borough and works for a computer company. His memories are also featured in Being There.

Was Saturday morning pictures noisy? Were the kids all shouting?

Oh yes, and we were all part of it and it's no good saying we weren't noisy. We were noisy. Everyone was noisy. But we used to get into the serials. That's the thing, that's what we used to go for - not so much the film that was on with it, because it was always like a cowboy that was on with it. We used to go for what will happen next week, how will he get out of it, and this was the beauty of it.

Did you have any favourite serials?

One which always stuck in my mind was *Undersea Kingdom*. We saw *Flash Gordon*, all this sort of thing, but *Undersea Kingdom* always stood in my mind. We had not the Three Musketeers - they were called the Three Mesquiteers, and that was three cowboys.

How did you know what was on?

We just took a chance and walked round to see what was outside - never read a paper to see what was what. We'd read up to see what films were coming out because everybody used to buy Picturegoer. You'd see what the film was, and the whole list of who was in it and who was playing who, but you used to know all the films.

And you'd look through that?

Yes, used to look through the lot, and then they'd give you a little write up on it and you'd say that seems a good film. You were taking their word all the time. And we used to look outside the cinemas and they would show just the still photographs, black-and-white, and you'd see a fellow with a gun and you'd say, "That looks a good film. Let's go and have some of that." And we'd go. Lovely.

Did you have favourite sorts of films? Did you go for Westerns?

When I was younger, I loved adventure films - naturally, being a boy. My favourite of all was adventure films and I still maintain the two best adventure films ever made were Errol Flynn in *The Sea Hawk* and Errol Flynn in *Robin Hood*.

One of the "two best adventure films ever made": Errol Flynn in The Adventures of Robin Hood *(1938) with Olivia de Havilland*

Did you and your friends talk about cinema a lot?

Not really. You went in and forgot about it. When you were younger children, you might fantasise a bit, like you'd go out and play and represent the Cowboys and Indians or whoever was the bad one. Tarzan films we used to go and see - I remember seeing Bruce Bennett as Tarzan. I used to love going to see Tarzan films, because you got a bit of light humour with Cheetah and all the rest.

Did you like thrillers and gangster films?

Loved them.

You liked James Cagney and Edward G. Robinson?

All of them. I liked character actors associated with them as well. Peter Lorre, Sydney Greenstreet with Bogart were just absolutely great.

And did you have particular stars you always wanted to see?

Not really. I loved all sorts of films. I'd go and see anything of Errol Flynn's because I really enjoyed Errol Flynn. Alan Ladd. When he started, you'd say, "There's an Alan Ladd film. That's a good film." You'd say it was a good film because Alan Ladd was in it.

What about female stars?

I wasn't really bothered. There was one I always liked and I thought she was beautiful: Paulette Goddard. She was always my favourite. Jane Withers. When I was a kid, my brother always used to gee me up about it: "You're in love with Jane Withers", like. I look at her now: she was plump and all the rest.

But you thought she was wonderful?

Yes. I used to like Linda Darnell but my wife always said she had boss eyes.

Did you have any favourites in the Fifties, like Tony Curtis perhaps?

Curtis - corr, the bee's knees. And Marlon Brando, and, of course, James Dean, although he wasn't around very long as we know. But I think Lex Barker and Rory Calhoun were my favourites because you used to be able to buy pictures of them in the arcades. In Brixton, they used to have shops with all pin-up photographs, black-and-white glossy pictures. Then, of course, pop music came along and ruined it. Everybody used to go on records.

Did you like musicals?

Musicals I loved. Gene Kelly, I thought was brilliant. And Dan Dailey and Donald O'Connor. And the likes of State Fair, which was an absolutely brilliant musical, with a good story.

What did you think of British films?

I didn't like British films. Not really. The actors were too plum in mouth. To me, they weren't real people. Whereas, when you got American films, even your little bit stars were

"The bee's knees": Tony Curtis

good. Here, if you had a bit star it would be a posh person trying to talk cockney. I liked Gordon Harker, Inspector Hornleigh, because he talked your language. Will Hay, Moore Marriott and Graham Moffatt, they were hysterical, lovely. The Crazy Gang we used to see - *Gasbags* and all that. They were funny. They were your sort of humour. But I could never really stand English English. In the War, you liked the war films.

People said that British films got better during the War - films like *The Way to the Stars* and *The Way Ahead* and *Millions Like Us*. They were still middle and upper class. I preferred to see Tommy Trinder in the one about the fire service.

A favourite: Rory Calhoun

The Bells Go Down.

Now I loved that. It was London. You were associating yourself with it. He did another one where he went to France and got all the children out.

The Foreman Went to France.

That was another one I used to like. Those sort of things I used to like. A lot of the other English ones, to me it always seemed that they were playing the piano or were blind. You had Ann Todd, she was always blind playing the piano. It seemed all we were seeing was Patricia Roc, Margaret Lockwood, Stewart Granger.

Eva O'Rourke

Eva O'Rourke, born in 1935 in Germany, saw her first film - an Andy Hardy comedy with Judy Garland - on the Isle of Man as a refugee. She now works as a librarian in Lambeth.

The cinemas I remember going to in Brixton are the Astoria, which is now a pop concert place, which used to have fish swimming around in a big pond in the middle with a fountain as you went in and all these balconies with arches and things like that, and the ABC which is now The Fridge. We occasionally went to a tiny cinema which is now called the Ritzy, but this had this fleapit reputation so we didn't go

there a lot. I used to go to the Trocadero as well because where I lived on Brixton Road you could go to the Elephant and Castle, a penny ha'penny the other way. It didn't have that horrible roundabout then, but I think the Elephant and Castle had a bit of a low reputation because we didn't go there a lot. And that had an organ and I would say I like the organ better than the fountains and stuff. I don't remember the Astoria having an organ but I know the Trocadero had.

Can you describe Saturday morning pictures?

To be honest, I didn't like it very much because there was this rough old queue and you didn't have any grown-ups and there was an awful lot of noise and you couldn't really hear the films, you couldn't get into them, and I was the sort of person who wanted to get lost in the romantic films. Often the features seemed to be Westerns which I didn't like at all. And when I was young they didn't have the special Children's Foundation films.

Olga San Juan with Billy De Wolfe in Variety Girl *(1947)*

What sort of films did you like?

I know I liked musicals and some stars of musicals. I liked Betty Grable, and Carmen Miranda. I used to like bright Technicolor things. I was too young to see the Busby Berkeleys first time round, but there was a certain sort of Twentieth Century-Fox big musical - *Diamond Horseshoe*, I remember. And I remember when I was coming home from Girl Guides - so I must have been ten or eleven - singing this little song I made up about Carmen Miranda.

Why did you like her?

She had a lovely personality. And she had all these bananery sorts of hats. Also, I had a slight foreign accent when I was little, and so did Carmen Miranda... foreign and lively. I also liked someone called Olga San Juan, who people don't remember very much. She used to double up with Billy de Wolfe and they had these spots in musicals, the sort of second lead spot. And for some reason I used to think it was ever so fashionable to have slicked-back black hair with a

parting in the middle and a sort of rose thing at the back. Olga San Juan and Carmen Miranda were both that sort of person. I liked Rita Hayworth as well.

You actually did your hair like that?

No, I had very short cut hair. I don't know why but in the War I always seemed to have my hair cut very short and you didn't have many clothes to go around and my brother couldn't wear my clothes but I had to wear his because he was about the same size for a boy which used to irritate me a lot.

So musicals were your big thing. Did you have any other kinds of films or stars you went for?

For some reason - I don't feel like that now - also Dorothy Lamour, with the sarong and the drawn-back black hair. Maybe it was the colour and the exoticness, the South Seas. They used to make films which were quite cheap but made in the South Seas with palm trees and singers and things. I'm

Location filming in a bombed building alongside the Thames with Harry Fowler in Hue and Cry *(1947)*

talking when I was eight, nine and ten, I used to like those things.

One film I particularly remember having to hang about asking to be taken in and waiting a long time was *Hue and Cry*. I really loved that film but it had a film on with it which was about a babysitter who got murdered or something like that and I could tell why I shouldn't have gone to see it because it upset me quite a lot.

Hue and Cry is the first film I remember thinking the plot was interesting, so I suppose I got slightly more into plots by then. But you always had a B movie on with the colourful movies and they would be cheap murder things where British Inspectors would work out murder mysteries so you got the plot there.

Yvonne Owen

But I did prefer the British films mainly because I thought you might see one of the stars somewhere. I used to write fan letters to every star, and you couldn't really write them to American ones because you didn't know the studio addresses. And I got an album where I've got very early pictures of people like Hazel Court and Petula Clark and Patricia Roc and Margaret Lockwood and Glynis Johns, and people like Yvonne Owen whom no one's ever heard of now. And I used to write. I used to get a magazine called Picturegoer, and Film Fun - that was a comic with film stars in it. In a lot of them, it would give the addresses of the studios and the addresses of the fan clubs and also you could buy packets of film star photos of most people. So I'd buy the packets of the American stars but the reason I liked the British pictures best was I used to like getting the individual replies from the stars.

So they wrote back. And did they also send a photograph?

Yes, they sent photographs individually signed because people didn't write to them very much. Especially people who were small stars like Yvonne Owen. I saw her in *Miranda*. I think she probably went and had her photograph taken in the studio and sent it to me with a little note saying she was glad that I liked her. I used to feel a bit mean sometimes saying that everybody was my favourite film star but, even out of those I did have, I liked them all or I wouldn't have written to them.

Did your friends do this letter writing?

No, it was a fairly solo sort of occupation. The other thing I used to really like, and I can't think why: most cinemas had panels outside them where they would have black-and-white stills, four on each of the panels, and I used to really like looking at those. I used to have a special feeling about them.

What about the male stars? Did you have a favourite?

Stewart Granger

Stewart Granger. I can't remember anybody else apart from people who had been in singing and dancing things as the leads. With people like Betty Grable, those sort of musicals, the leading man wasn't significant at all - they never danced or anything, they just hung around and married them in the end. But I liked Stewart Granger very much. I was very jealous of Jean Simmons because she was this little girl who came from a background like me and roughly of the same age and she suddenly got into films and married Stewart Granger. I supposed I liked Griffith Jones a bit but that was because he was in *Miranda* and I thought *Miranda* was a very romantic film for some reason.

When I was eighteen, I became an usherette because I loved the cinema so much and I needed a job. I was an usherette at a cinema called the Tivoli in the Strand which has gone now. We had a lot of first-run films. Although it was a West End cinema, it wasn't quite West End. I used to go after school and so it must have been from five to closing time. And I used to sell ice creams. You were an ice cream person or an usherette. I know that when you sold ice cream you earned a bit more money for doing that, but if the ice cream melted you used to have to pay for it. It always would melt. I think they did it on purpose. You didn't know whether to be an ice-cream person or not, because you got to finish earlier and you didn't have to do so much.

Did they have big openings with stars?

Not very major ones. It was sub-West End. It seemed to have things on only for one week or two weeks. The biggest thing I can remember having an opening was something with Tony Wright who disappeared soon afterwards. He played a boxer. It was a British film [*The Flanagan Boy*, 1953]. And because it wasn't a success and nobody had ever heard of him afterwards, he used to come to the Tivoli and we would say, "Oh, there's Tony Wright!" It was the only place he could have that.

I saw films there that I remember very well I wouldn't have gone out to see, which I wouldn't have thought I would like. *Gilbert and Sullivan*: Robert Morley walks off and the other one dies and he's alone. I used to think that was sad.

Was it quite common, do you think, for usherettes to be film fans?

They probably wouldn't have taken the job because they were film fans - because jobs were jobs, but it made it a lot nicer if you were interested in the film. But at the same time it was difficult because if you wanted to watch the film you'd get into trouble. There used to be favourite bits that I'd want to see and not be disturbed on. And because I was doing it after school, often when people had come in for the last film and nobody came in after that, I would sit on one of those little flip-down seats at the back doing my homework by the light of the torch, all wobbly writing.

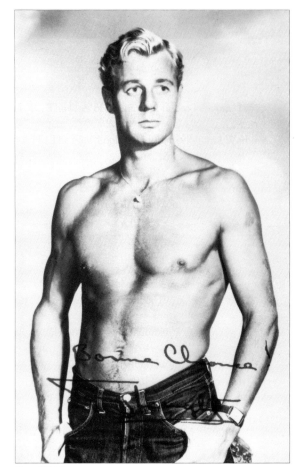

Tony Wright

Suzanne Waite

Suzanne Waite, born in Walworth in 1937, recalls her early years around the Elephant and Castle. Her memories also appear in Being There.

Every time I went was special to me because I really fancied myself in the pictures. Every time I watched one of these films, especially if there were children in it, I wished it was me up there. I loved it. There was nothing ever more special any other time. I just loved going to the cinema.

Did you have a preference for particular types of films?

Musicals and sad ones were my favourites. Musicals were my great love. Any musical. I used to go and see them so many times. I'd say to my dad, "Can we go and see that?" And he'd say, "You've seen it once." "Well, can I go on up on my own and watch it?" "No. Oh, all right, I'll take you."

Did you have any favourite stars?

Margaret Lockwood. I adored her. And Pat Roc. But I think my greatest one was Judy Garland and, as I got older,

Margaret Lockwood with James Mason in The Wicked Lady *(1945)*

Marilyn Monroe. Judy Garland died in this country and they put her in a glass coffin and I wanted to see that but my husband wouldn't let me go.

Which male stars of the Forties did you like?

Humphrey Bogart. I liked Alan Ladd but I was very disappointed when I found out how small he was. We could never see that in films. The one I hated most was Randolph Scott. He used to wear a terrible hat. I hated Westerns. But I think best were the English stars - James Mason, Stewart Granger.

Everybody liked Stewart Granger.

But he was always the rotter, wasn't he? That's why everybody liked him.

Did films and stars have an influence on you or the people you knew?

I think everybody used to try and dress like the stars of the time.

Did you prefer British or American films generally?

I felt British actors and actresses were more serious. We had all the good stories but most musicals then were American musicals, except for Anna Neagle - she made some lovely musicals.

Did you enjoy British comedies that dealt with the War?

There was one at the end of War, *Passport to Pimlico* - we used to watch that being made as kids, we used to all run round there to watch that being made.

Margaret Lockwood

What about British war films?

In Which We Serve, I remember that one. *Millions Like Us*. *The Way to the Stars* - Rosamund John. There was the Warsaw Concerto in one. Where we lived in this block of flats - in the flat below there was a very nice family and their son was in the War. When he came home, he would play the piano, he used to play the Warsaw Concerto. I remember my mum so upset one day. He'd been killed.

Did you prefer films that had nothing to do with the War?

Yes. I didn't likewar films at all. I never enjoyed them. I think we had enough of it. I liked musicals. I used to love the Lassie films. Lassie, I would cry.

I used to love all Margaret Lockwood's films, *The Wicked Lady*, and all those American musicals. I used to come home and dance to my dad. As I got older, one I really enjoyed seeing was *Mandy* - Mandy Miller, she was deaf and dumb. I was so attracted to that, I would sit and break my heart all the way through that. I kept on going to see it.

"I would sit and break my heart": Mandy Miller in Mandy (1952)

Mo Heard

Mo Heard, born in 1940, went into acting as a career and is now in charge of the Actors' Company at the Museum of the Moving Image. She is also interviewed in Being There and Working There.

Did you read film magazines?

At some point I discovered Picture Show and Picturegoer and I would go into the newsagents and buy those every week. And I was gripped by these magazines. I would pore over these photographs of stars and read the story of their lives and their wonderful families and their gardens and their houses and their swimming pools, and I just loved those magazines.

But it was also the annuals. You'd go about November into

"I was in love with Audie Murphy until..."

the local newsagents - I don't remember ever going into a bookshop then, it was newsagents - and they'd have all the film annuals and all the various other children's annuals on a shelf. I would look at them and I would drool and have to have those books. And I had them every Christmas - I got Picture Show Annual, Film Review ... what other annuals were there?

As I got older - round about twelve or thirteen - I was

Four stars and the Picturegoer Seal of Merit for Invasion of the Body Snatchers *(1956)*

absolutely obsessed by film stars, really more than the films. I started cutting pictures out of Picturegoer and Picture Show instead of just keeping the magazines and just looking at them. It was magic to cut the pictures out of Doris Day or Rory Calhoun. Cameron Mitchell - I loved him. Audie Murphy...my god, I was in love with Audie Murphy until I found out he was only about five feet tall.

What did you do with the cuttings?

I stuck the pictures in scrapbooks. And I had lots of scrapbooks. And then in the back of - was it Picturegoer? - you could send off for glossy postcard photographs - a brown sort of sepia - and I would save up and send away for those. I would stick them into my scrapbook.

And one thing about Picturegoer: they had crits of the films each week and they would have a star system, four stars for an excellent film, and three and two and one. One film which got four stars was *Invasion of the Body Snatchers*. I had to go and see that.

Then the other magazine was ABC Film Review. It was sixpence, I think, and it came out once a month. Every time I went to the Plaza at Catford, I always insisted on having it.

When I was a bit older, probably fifteen, I went to Aske's [school] in New Cross and I found another friend there who was also interested in the cinema. And during the holidays we used to write a whole story to each other with film titles in the story. And so each of us had to find the hidden titles

Dorothy Bromiley (left) with Joan Elan and Audrey Dalton in The Girls of Pleasure Island *(1953)*

in the story. And I'd go through all my old Picturegoers and Picture Shows and take titles that seemed to say they would be interesting in a story. The idea was to find really obscure ones which my friend Clare wouldn't ever spot. So you'd find titles like *She* - one word titles. This was great. We used to do this every holiday.

Aske's was a girls' grammar school and the headmistress absolutely, categorically, stated that no girl was allowed to bring in magazines to school. I think it was to do with the fact that a lot of girls brought in all the women's magazines - Woman's Own, and all those trashy magazines. And I remember I was so desperate to get Picturegoer or Picture Show as soon as they came out that I had to get it on my way to school. And I'd bury it at the bottom of my satchel and

never brought it out because I used to try and keep to any rules and regulations. But that whole thing of knowing that pristine magazine was in my satchel and I couldn't wait until I got home to read it!

I remember once I was in bad books, flicking ink or something over a teacher, and I was hauled up in front of the headmistress and she obviously thought I was a case for Borstal or something. And she started quizzing me about all sorts of things and she said, "Do you bring magazines into the school?" Now, me being so honest, I could have said no but I said yes, I did. And that was the final straw as far as she was concerned. At that age you don't feel like saying, "They're at the bottom of my satchel. I never bring them out and I never read them in school." I always remember that, being so honest. And then I was suspended for three days.

I remember that there was a film going to be made about four American sailors and it was set on an island in the Pacific. And there were three or four sisters and they had to be English and there was a whole nationwide search for these new actresses. And this was in the Picturegoer, all the film mags. Dorothy Bromiley was the English girl chosen to be in this film. Can you imagine - with someone like Gene Barry, who I thought was absolutely wonderful, and there was this English girl, I think she worked for Joe Lyons, and she'd been chosen to be in this film! I couldn't have been more jealous.

I remember loving the ads and all those trailers. There is one particular advertising film I remember. Perhaps it was once a month or something. It was like a mini-film about household tips and it was all in Technicolor. If anybody could send in a household tip like putting a rubber band round a stiff jar top, silly things like that, they won £25. And you'd see these £5 notes which this person was winning spread out on the screen.

When I was seventeen or eighteen, I started coming to the National Film Theatre. I think the first time I came to the NFT was when they had that big Ingmar Bergman season. I'd never heard of him. I thought he was wonderful. And then they had a brilliant season about that time called Beat, Square and Cool with John Cassavetes' *Shadows* and I think that was when I realised there were interesting films being made.

Allen Eyles

Allen Eyles, born in 1941, was brought up in Tooting Bec and Streatham. He became a teacher and then a film historian, developing a specialist interest in cinema buildings. He also contributes to Being There.

Did you go to Saturday morning pictures?

Basically, I hated Saturday morning pictures because it was meant for kids and I didn't want to be associated with it. I wanted to see films that adults were seeing. But I went to the Astoria Brixton one Saturday morning because there was a Hopalong Cassidy film on and I'd never seen one and I found it was just a dreadful B Western. I wished I hadn't gone.

I remember seeing Laurel and Hardy in *Jailbirds* at the Rex Norbury one Saturday morning and the print was in a shocking condition, one of the worst prints I've ever seen. It was just full of jumps and scratches and everything. But I really thought it was insulting to show these bad films, either bad in content or bad in print condition, to children and take money off them for it.

Once I went to the Regal Streatham for a Saturday morning and I had to enroll and I was given my ABC Minors badge and I was told to sit in a certain section of the rear stalls under a prefect and I was supposed to sing the ABC song. The prefect was just an older boy who was given the responsibility of trying to keep some semblance of order in that section of the cinema. It was like being in school. Then the cinema manager would masquerade as your Uncle Arthur or something. I just didn't like that. I was much happier seeing films at other times.

You fell in love with cinema when you were about eleven?

Yes. I bought copies of the fan magazines almost straight away, Picturegoer and Picture Show. Picturegoer was much livelier and I only bought one copy of Picture Show before deciding in favour of Picturegoer. I particularly enjoyed its review section which I found very readable. I placed an order for it with a newsagent and used that as a way of learning about films. I saved up to buy Maurice Speed's Western Film Annual and later his annual Film Review as well.

On top of that, I had at that time a new bicycle and used to go cycling all over the place. I quite often passed cinemas like the Clapham Pavilion which had a big display of posters for films that used to be either Westerns with Randolph Scott or swashbucklers with Cornel Wilde. And I would make a note of what was coming up. Or I would pick up the programmes from cinemas which they issued each month. I'd seen *Bicycle Thieves* and I never dared lock up my bicycle and go and see the films while I was cycling around in case it was nicked.

I found that the older cinemas offered better value for money because you usually got two good films in the programme and didn't have to pay as much to get in. I remember, for example, going to the Granada Tooting and seeing a Burt Lancaster Foreign Legion escapade called *Ten Tall Men*. I didn't enjoy going to the Granada that much - I was whisked to my seat and plonked down on the side near the front and had a rather bad view of the screen. And in support of *Ten Tall Men* there was just a boring Gene Autry B Western that I didn't enjoy at all. I felt more at home in places like the Vogue and the Classic, the other repertory cinema at Tooting Bec which did slightly more sophisticated films, Bob Hope comedies like *My Favourite Spy*. Those cinemas I went to a lot.

Did you always go on your own?

Usually to the older films, yes, because I didn't know anyone who really wanted to go and see them with me. And most of my friends didn't see any point in going a long way to see films. Sometimes when I wanted to see an "A" certificate film my mother would go with me and I saw an awful lot of Robert Mitchum films with her. Her real favourite, she told me far too late to do anything about it, was Franchot Tone, not that there were that many Franchot Tone films around in my youth. She was also very fond of Fernandel in the Don Camillo films and I got her to take me to see another Fernandel film called *The Sheep Has Five Legs*, which she tut-

tutted about afterwards because it had one or two risqué moments.

My father would take me and my younger brother and sister sometimes to films as a kind of family outing. He would take us to Norman Wisdom comedies and *Doctor in the House* films that he thought we would enjoy, and my mum would come to those, too. Then he would often take me to War films. I know he had the feeling that we boys should be aware of the Second World War and the sacrifices that had been made, that it would be good for us to know something about it. We went to *Angels One Five* as a family on holiday in Margate and to *Reach for the Sky* as a last resort when it poured with rain on a wet day out to Brighton. He took me to *The Malta Story*, *The Dam Busters*, *Cockleshell Heroes*, *Bridge on the River Kwai*...all the big hits that used to come along about once a year that he heard of. I think the last one he ever took me to was *Dunkirk*.

Fernandel (centre)with a provocative Lina Lopez in The Sheep Has Five Legs

So you sometimes saw new films with friends from school?

If groups went together from school, it was usually to films that didn't particularly interest me - occasionally I would tag along. I remember once some friends came round the house and said they were going to see a film which didn't interest me so I said, "I won't bother." I spoke to them the next day and it turned out they'd gone and seen Brigitte Bardot in *And Woman...Was Created*. And I said, "Why didn't you tell me you were going to see that!" They said, "We didn't like to mention it in front of your mother."

Did every schoolboy have an ambition to go and see a Bardot film?

Well, there was this whole business of getting into "X" certificate films, which meant horror first and, a bit later on, sex. Obviously I couldn't get into "X" films very easily when I was in short trousers and only twelve or thirteen. I do remember the Vogue Tooting had a double bill of John Carradine in *The Corpse Vanished* and I think it was George Zucco in *Dead Men Walk*. I really felt very tempted and I marched up to the paybox and the cashier was very polite and said she would like to let me in but would I mind going home and just letting her see my birth certificate. So that squashed that.

When we went on holiday to Margate I used to get fed up sitting on the beach and go off and wander round. And somewhere on the edge of the town I found a cinema which was showing not one "X" film, not two, but three "X" films in the same programme: *Abbott and Costello Meet Dr. Jekyll and Mr. Hyde*, *Life After Dark* and a cartoon version of *The Tell Tale Heart*. I thought this was too good to miss so I'd give it a try. I wasn't really planning to go to the cinema and had to be back for tea, but I just tried it out and to my surprise they let me in. It must have been a sunny afternoon and they were so desperate for customers they'd let anybody in. I saw this dreary juvenile delinquency drama, *Life After Dark*, with that great star Harvey Lembeck. I couldn't see why it was an "X" because I'd seen "A" films which were no worse than this. *The Tell Tale Heart* didn't frighten me particularly but it was a fairly interesting version of the Poe story. I saw a bit of the

Harvey Lembeck (left), Jaclynne Greene, Patricia Hardy, Glen Roberts and Joyce Holden in the 'X' certificate drama, Life After Dark

Abbott and Costello and then I had to leave. Horror films certainly had a fascination for boys of that age.

Sex films? A group from school went down to a rather seedy cinema in Tooting called the Astoria. They always had a big poster outside headed "Your Favourite Astoria" - but whose favourite Astoria it could possibly have been when there was a much better one a mile or so down the road in Streatham I have no idea. But it played sensational pictures from time to time. And we went down to see this Brigitte Bardot picture with subtitles, *The Light Across the Street*. Everyone was fidgety and noisy, then complete silence fell over the auditorium when Bardot unbuttoned her blouse.

Did you collect images from films?

Yes. When I was about twelve, I remember wandering around the West End and I found Wardour Street. I wandered up and down looking at the various displays of forthcoming films in the windows of the distributors there. There was a company called Eros Films which specialised in reissues of old, big Hollywood films and the doorman allowed me to quickly take four of the many brochures I could see on display - I got ones for *Pride and Prejudice, Five Graves to Cairo*...I can't remember the other two. And I asked for any spare leaflets at the Associated British Pathe office and a secretary kindly took down my name and address and sent me a fat

envelope full of press handouts for films like *House of the Arrow* and *South of Algiers*.

Later I discovered that the library in West Norwood took the trade paper, the Kine Weekly, and I found out they would sell them off cheap after a while. I used to cycle over there every four or six weeks and buy up for a nominal sum all these recent Kine Weeklies and devour the information in them. And also they used to have full-page colour adverts, usually for more obscure films, that I would tear out and pin up in my bedroom as posters. We had a lodger who used to help my mother and clean my room and she complained about one of these posters and said, "Is this a nice thing for a boy to have in his room?" So I went and looked at what it was she was on about - it was an advert for a boxing film called *Champ for a Day* starring Alex Nicol, and the wording across the top was "His Fists Made for Killing! Her Lips Made for Kissing!" I couldn't justify myself but I refused to take it down. It made me aware that some aspects of films weren't too respectable.

Brigitte Bardot in The Light Across the Street (1955) *with Raymond Pellegrin*

Did you have obsessions about particular stars?

I'd gone through stages of collecting stamps and matchbox labels and comics like The Wizard and Adventure and I started, I think, to collect films with particular stars in. Most films that I saw with Gary Cooper I enjoyed anyway. I saw films because John Wayne was in them, like *Trouble Along the*

Way which was a romantic comedy-drama despite its title, which I wouldn't have wanted to see otherwise. I set out to see all the Marx Brothers films and I compiled a list of them all and ticked them off as I saw them. I wasn't so keen on female stars though I did have a strong liking for Dorothy McGuire and Maureen O'Hara.

I kept notes on all the films that I saw and started giving them star ratings as Picturegoer did. Eventually I started doing these books, drawing coloured advertisements for the films I saw. I copied the style of the posters in various coloured inks and I would do an advert for each film and stick on it how I rated it. After a while I found one to four stars wasn't flexible enough, so I started rating films out of ten - but I never gave anything ten.

Was this all separate from school?

Yes, I was never really encouraged to like films as much as I did. My parents who both wore glasses said that it would ruin my eyesight which it never did. My brother and sister ended up wearing glasses and they never went much to the cinema. I developed a theory that going to the cinema on hot

Eros Films brochure for reissued Five Graves to Cairo

sunny days and resting my eyes in a cool, dark environment was the best thing I could do for my eyesight.

I was made to feel that going to the cinema wasn't that desirable, but my parents had to give in to it as long as my school marks didn't suffer - which they didn't. The big sticking point was Sundays when the cinemas showed old films that I was really keen to see and my father was adamant that I shouldn't go to the cinema on Sundays. He wasn't conventionally religious but he just didn't think it was the right thing to do.

I remember there was a Gary Cooper film called *Souls at Sea* at the Granada Thornton Heath which I was desperate to see and I couldn't get him to let me go, although I did see a John Wayne film called *Big Jim McLain* on a Sunday at the

Brixton Palladium, which must have been on the sly. I spent so much money getting there I bought the cheapest seats and it was so crowded that I ended up in the front row. I couldn't take in the film, the screen was so close.

What about your teachers?

The only encouragement I got was from a trainee teacher called Geduld. I am very grateful to him because he loaned me a book - Lewis Jacobs' *The Rise of the American Film* - and actually said "You ought to read this and develop your interest in film." And in the Sixth Form we had a French conversation teacher and he was very keen on films and I remember him talking about Renoir's *Le Déjeuner sur l'Herbe* and the New Wave films that were coming along at that time. And he encouraged us to see these. I remember seeing *Les Quatre Cents Coups* at the Curzon. And we saw *Les Cousins* and other early French Nouvelle Vague films. And we would then retire, usually to a coffee bar called Le Macabre in Soho which was basically slabs like tombstones in a basement with skulls and crossbones. We sat there and solemnly discussed the film before lapsing into idle chatter.

When did your family get television?

I would say shortly after the Coronation. We didn't have a television set at the time but anyone who had one entertained whole hordes of neighbours and I think it made a lot of people resolve to get one. We got one that had BBC and then of course when ITV came in you had to get your set adjusted or get a new one. We didn't have ITV for a long time. There was a family friend who had ITV and I got quite excited because they were showing all these old Warner Bros. films on Saturday nights. I arranged to see one, George Raft in *They Drive By Night*. I went along to watch it but at ten o'clock on the dot the man switched the set off and said, "We go to bed at ten o'clock here." So I was very frustrated by this and couldn't see the end of the film.

When did you leave school?

At the end of the Fifties. Then I went to the London School of Economics. I was still an avid filmgoer. I became very active in the Film Society at the LSE. I did posters for films in my first year there and after that I did some

programming. I got involved in student journalism and managed to get tickets to press shows in the West End.

I never used to go to the West End ordinarily as a boy because my parents never thought of going there and I knew that the films would come down to Streatham before too long. One exception I can recall was John Wayne in the 3-D *Hondo* at the Warner Leicester Square. I went to that early on the very first day when they had a reduced admission price and I sat through it twice because of all the effort I'd made to get there and it was still expensive.

Then later on *The Searchers* came along. I went on the day that opened and saw the first and second performances. I remember thinking that I was the first person along with the others in the auditorium to see the film in Britain and I got a

bit of a kick out of that. *The Searchers* made a tremendous impression on me and I saw it again when it came round to the Regal Streatham.

Were you particularly keen on Westerns?

Oh yes, I always enjoyed Westerns, and adventure films. One of the first films I saw was a revival of *Lives of a Bengal Lancer* with Gary Cooper at the Picture House Balham, and I made a point of seeing that kind of film when it came around. I think I liked most types of films but, not having a good ear for music, I wasn't terribly taken with musicals. I didn't like a lot of British films because they basically were too talkative and the characters didn't interest me.

When did you first become interested in the cinemas themselves?

I cycled around a lot and I carried my camera as I was interested in photography. There was a very modern-looking Odeon cinema on a roundabout at Elmers End that used to fascinate me as nobody ever seemed to be going into it. I took some photographs of that after it closed. And I passed the Savoy in York Road, Wandsworth, as I had once or twice

The Elephant and Castle Trocadero at the time of closure in 1963

before, but this time they were in the process of pulling it down, so I stopped and took a few photographs, wishing I had gone inside while it was still open.

Then I remember learning that the Trocadero at the

Elephant and Castle was going to close. This was a huge cinema I'd often cycled past. But this was the first time I really felt that I had to go and see a place while it was still open. I remember watching in the paper for something tolerable to see there and it was showing a James Mason comedy called *A Touch of Larceny*. I made a point of trekking out to the Elephant and even sat through the whole programme to get the flavour of the place. There was a dreadful B film called *Night Train to Inverness* which was the kind of film I was avoiding at the time.

I had developed the habit of missing the B film, unless I'd heard it was any good, of missing the news which never particularly interested me,

Early cinema photographs: 'a very modern looking Odeon' at Elmers End...

of missing the advertising which always came before the news, and coming in some time during the trailers which I always enjoyed and then seeing the main film. But on this occasion at the Trocadero I sat through the whole programme. There was definitely an impressive atmosphere about the place. I sat on the huge stalls floor and they had sequinned curtains where they flooded it with light in the intervals so that they sparkled and the music they played seemed to add to the atmosphere. There were quite a lot of people there, so the place was very inviting. I made a point of going there two or three times more, sitting in the circle, before it closed.

When you were at the LSE involved in the Film Society, what sort of things did the students go for?

We showed some of the conventional film society things -

Ingmar Bergmans and things of that sort - but I would throw in a few gangster films and odd choices to stir things up a bit. The entertainment was so cheap you got big crowds in whatever you showed. I remember once the film didn't turn up and I had to arrange an emergency substitute. I got hold of a French comedy I particularly liked called *Vive Monsieur Blaireau* and duplicated some leaflets and left them all around the dining area. I chose the film without consulting the rest of the committee but it went down quite well.

Did you have to argue for your choice of films?

Oh yes. I remember getting films like the Gregory Peck Western *The Gunfighter* and Rod Steiger's *Al Capone* put on because I said they were good. Nobody knew them to argue otherwise. It used to be a kind of voting system on the committee. A friend of mine said, "If you vote for my Bergman I'll vote for your *Al Capone*." That was the way films got selected. I designed the programme leaflet for the Film Society, so I put *Al Capone* on the cover. I had my own way in that.

What has been so special about film-going for you?

...and demolition of the Savoy, York Road, Wandsworth

I don't think it's the film-going itself so much as the actual films. I very rarely got completely bored with films. I've only ever walked out of a handful of films, mostly foreign ones that I just couldn't stand any more, like *Eve Wants to Sleep*. I think what is important about going to the cinema is that you commit yourself to seeing that film and you surrender to it and see how well it works on you, whereas if you're watching a film on television or video, you're not watching it as intently because you've always got a choice of switching it off or you might be interrupted by the phone ringing.

Tony Sloman

Tony Sloman, born in 1945, works as a film editor and has arranged seasons at the National Film Theatre. His memories are also recorded in Being There.

I was five when I moved to Streatham. The first film I remember seeing in Streatham was *King Solomon's Mines*. It was just wonderful. I discovered a hero. I wanted to be Allan Quartermain. I wanted to cavort in the jungle, not so much with Deborah Kerr, but I wanted to dress like him and have white sideburns and be that bronzed. He was absolutely a

"Absolutely a hero figure": Stewart Granger (right) in King Solomon's Mines *(1950) with Richard Carlson and Deborah Kerr*

hero figure. And, as luck would have it, since I was only taken to films which were considered "suitable", I ended up seeing most of Stewart Granger's films of that period. He was my favourite film star.

As a special treat for my birthday or in school holidays if I'd done well, I was taken up West to see a film and I used to get What's On and see what had opened. And, of course, the biggest treat, as you can imagine, was an "A"-certificated film starring Stewart Granger. *The Last Hunt* was what I wanted to see for my birthday, May 6. And that was the beginning of

"Marvellous scene": the fencing climax of Scaramouche (1952) *with Stewart Granger*

seeing two films a day: that was when I saw *The Last Hunt* in the evening and *Richard III* during the day. I went to see *Richard III* at the Astoria Streatham and that terrified me, it really terrified me: the ghosts before the battle, the only time I ever remember cowering under my seat.

The revelation of my picture-going years was *Scaramouche* in 1952. I didn't know the story. I saw *Ivanhoe* and I'd read *Ivanhoe* as a Classic Illustrated so I knew the plot. *Scaramouche* I wasn't ready for. I wasn't ready for the style, the humour, what I now perceive to be wit but then I just thought very funny. I didn't know at the time it had the longest fencing scene ever, and it was just this marvellous scene with Stewart Granger and Mel Ferrer. So my hero was involved in one of my own favourite films.

You can imagine my delight when I discovered that Stewart Granger's birthday was May 6, same as mine. I saw all the Stewart Granger films that were considered suitable: *Young Bess, The Prisoner of Zenda*. It seemed after a while that he was the only one I was taken to see, apart from Richard Todd. Having seen *Robin Hood*, I saw *Rob Roy* and that was the first time I went to a cinema on a Friday night. I badgered and harangued my parents. My mother wouldn't go. My father took me to see *Rob Roy* and I remember vividly that it was a Friday night. I thought I would be awfully punished for not being at home on Shabat evening.

Did that set a precedent?

Once I wasn't punished, I realised this could work because my father, who was a tailor, finished early on Friday nights, so we could probably try it again. It was the week of Sunday January 16, 1955. *The Student Prince* and *The Barefoot Contessa* went out on release the same week. I wanted to see *The Barefoot Contessa* because Humphrey Bogart and Ava Gardner were to me, at ten, much more exciting than Edmund Purdom and Ann Blyth. But, of course, *The Student Prince* was "suitable". If you know the plot of *The Barefoot Contessa*, which my parents must have done, it's really not at all suitable because it deals with an illegitimate child and impotence and all sorts of things I wouldn't understand. But I was terrible. I threw tantrums and went to see *The Barefoot Contessa*. We came in the middle - we always did - and saw it round again. It couldn't have made any sense to me, or indeed anyone else, seen that way - but I'd seen *The Barefoot Contessa* and it was an "A" so I'd managed to get people to take me.

Rock Hudson was a major hero. Nobody knew that he was homosexual. Rock Hudson was tall and good-looking, and what a movie star. I was desperate to see *Magnificent Obsession* but my father said, "We'll go to the Boys and Girls Exhibition at Olympia", and we did. I was very annoyed about that. I'll never forget missing *Magnificent Obsession* that time to see trains go round. He was probably right. I wouldn't have understood it. But Hudson was major.

And that was the next wave after Granger - the so-called beef-cake wave which included Tony Curtis and Jeff Chandler. I used to see a lot of Jeff Chandler, who is forgotten now. He was a big movie star, a good-looking movie star. Of course, he was Jewish and the other thing in my family which was important was to watch out for Jewish movie stars. I knew who were Jewish movie stars. I knew that Edward G. Robinson who I'd hardly seen was the son of a Rabbi somewhere. And I knew that Kirk Douglas was Issur Demsky and Jeff Chandler was Ira Grossel, and we were very proud of our Jewish movie stars. And I remember thinking that maybe movies were more important than religion and school and family. But then I was seeing so many. I was bombarded by them.

Jewish movie star: Jeff Chandler

Whoever put out *Love Me Tender* with an "A" as its support deserved to be hung and quartered. I can tell you what was on with it. Fox had a series of short remakes, pocket editions. It was *Laura*. And Elvis was God. I was getting over Stewart

Elvis Presley in Love Me Tender *(1956) with Mildred Dunnock and William Campbell*

Granger. Elvis was the all-time hero. I waited outside the Clifton Brixton Hill and I couldn't get to see *Love Me Tender*. People used to ask people to take them in and I just waited - I couldn't bring myself to ask these people to take me in. So I

Stewart Granger in his last swashbuckling movie, The Swordsman of Siena *(1961)*

never saw *Love Me Tender* on its first release.

If that wasn't bad enough, *Jailhouse Rock* had an "A". I couldn't get to see *Jailhouse Rock* either. And then it was endless. *Loving You* went out with *Short Cut to Hell*, which was an "A", at the Gaumont Streatham. Eventually I caught up with *Love Me Tender* with *MacDonald of the Canadian Mounties* at the Brixton Pullman, and *Jailhouse Rock* at the Classic Stockwell where I used to go twice a week if I could. By that time I knew of the existence of other cinemas like the Cameo Victoria and going to Victoria was a big adventure but that's where I finally caught up with *Loving You*. *King Creole* was an "A". I was still too young to see *King Creole* on release and saw it eventually at the Granada Tooting - I think, in a double bill with *Last Train from Gun Hill*. And after that I saw every single Elvis movie consecutively as they deteriorated.

When I finally left Dulwich, that afternoon, my best friend Nick Nash and I, we went to see a double bill which symbolised, I guess, the end of our childhood. It was a double bill of Elvis in *It Happened at the World's Fair*, which was probably the beginning of his decline, and the second half of

the double bill was Stewart Granger in *Swordsman of Siena*, which was the last swashbuckling movie he ever made.

When did you first see "X" films?

I had a bus pass - you had half fares when you were fourteen and I got my form master to sign the bus pass and I had my thumb over the space for the age. So, after he'd signed it, I took it to my desk and wrote "16" so that I could go to "X" films.

My first "X" film, I suppose typically of the films of my generation, had to be Brigitte Bardot. I was desperate. I had that life-size picture that Reveille published on my bedroom door along with all the other film posters, and I was just desperate to see her. I'd seen *Doctor at Sea* and absolutely fell for her. This was just major. I'd missed *And Woman … Was Created* and here was *Heaven Fell That Night* and there was a chance that would be my first "X". And I went to see it and

Brigitte Bardot and Stephen Boyd in Heaven Fell That Night *(1958)*

B movie which was directed by Max Varnel. I can't remember what it was called. And the process - I was obsessed with processes: colour, and what particular 'scope and stereo system - and then my rating.

I'll never, ever, forget those wonderful old certificates with a great big "X". It was wonderful. And the film was pretty good, too.

Had your reading changed?

Yes, I read Films and Filming instead of Picturegoer. There was a friend of mine at school, David Trace, and he said, "You've got to read Films and Filming. Picture Show and Picturegoer are really just rubbish." And, yes, he was right, but Picturegoer taught me ratings and I have written down ever since *Easter Parade* every single film I've seen and still do, including cartoons and shorts, everything seen on screen. I don't count television. And I rate it - and this is a really eccentric thing that a lot of other people do - zero to five. And I find sometimes I might upgrade a few, but generally after I go back and see them after thirty years the first rating was spot on.

I didn't write a critical list. I went into directors about 1962/63. The first film I ever listed the director was a British

Bibliography

Aldgate A. and Richards J., Britain Can Take It. Oxford, Basil Blackwell, 1986.

Atwell D., Cathedrals of the Movies: a History of British Cinemas and their Audiences. London, Architectural Press, 1980.

Beddoe D., Back to Home and Duty. London, Pandora, 1989.

Breakwell I. and Hammond P., Seeing in the Dark. London, Serpent's Tail, 1990.

Calder A., The People's War. London, Penguin, 1971.

Chamberlain E., 29 Inman Road. London, Virago, 1990.

Chamberlain M., Growing up in Lambeth. London, Virago, 1989.

Croall J., Don't You Know There's a War On? London, Hutchinson, 1990.

Curran J. and Porter V., British Cinema History. London, Weidenfeld and Nicholson, 1983.

Doherty D., Morrison D. and Tracey M., The Last Picture Show? Britain's Changing Film Audiences. London, 1987.

Durgnat R., A Mirror for England. London, Faber and Faber, 1970.

Eyles A. and Skone K., The Cinemas of Croydon. Surrey, Keytone, 1991.

Eyles A. and Skone K., London's West End Cinemas. Surrey, Keytone, 1991.

Field A., The Picture Palace: A Social History of the Cinema. London, 1974.

Graves R. and Hodge A., The Long Weekend: a Social History of Great Britain 1918-39. London, Hutchinson, 1985.

Halliwell L., Seats in All Parts. London, Grafton Books, 1985.

Hoggart R., The Uses of Literacy. London, Penguin, 1957.

Hopkins H., The New Look. London, Secker and Warburg, 1963.

Humphries S. and Taylor T., The Making of Modern London 1945-85. London, Sidgwick and Jackson, 1986.

Low R., Film Making in 1930s Britain. London, Allen and Unwin, 1985.

Low R., 'The Implications behind the Social Survey', Penguin Film Review 7, September 1948

Mack J. and Humphreys S., London at War. London, Sidgwick and Jackson, 1985.

Manvell R., The Film and the Public. Harmondsworth, Penguin, 1955.

Marwick A., British Society since 1945. Harmondsworth, Penguin, 1982.

Mayer J. P., British Cinemas and their Audiences. London, Denis Dobson, 1948.

Mayer J. P., Sociology of the Film. London, Faber and Faber, 1946.

Morgan G., Red Roses Every Night: an Account of London's Cinemas Under Fire. London, Quality Press, 1948.

Murphy R., Realism and Tinsel. London, Routledge, 1989.

Richards J.,The Age of the Dream Palace. London, Routledge, 1984.

Richards J. and Sheridan D. (eds.), Mass Observation at the Movies. London, Routledge, 1987.

Richards J. and Aldgate A., British Cinema and Society 1930-1970. Oxford, Basil Blackwell, 1983.

Sharp D., The Picture Palace and Other Buildings for the Movies. London, Hugh Evelyn, 1969.

Sorlin P., European Cinemas, European Societies 1939-1990 London, Routledge, 1991.

Stead P., Film and the Working Class. London, Routledge, 1989.

Swann P., The Hollywood Feature Film in Postwar Britain. London, Croom Helm, 1987.

Taylor H., Scarlett's Women: Gone with the Wind and its Female Fans. London, Virago, 1989.

Taylor P. M. (ed.), Britain and the Cinema in the Second World War. London, Macmillan, 1988.

Thompson P., The Voice of the Past. London, Oxford University Press, 1978.

Webb M., Greater London's Suburban Cinemas. Birmingham, Amber Valley, 1986.

Wood L., British Film Industry. London, British Film Institute, 1980.

Index

Cinemas are usually listed under their locations. Numbers in italics refer to illustrations